Splatter Capital: The Political Economy of Gore Films

Splatter Capital:
The Political
Economy of
Gore Films

Mark Steven

Published by Repeater Books
An imprint of Watkins Media Ltd
19–21 Cecil Court
London
WC2N 4EZ
UK

www.repeaterbooks.com

A Repeater Books paperback original 2017
1

Distributed in the United States by Random House,
Inc., New York.

Cover design: Johnny Bull
Typography and typesetting: Josse Pickard
Typefaces: Akko Rounded Pro/TheSerif

ISBN: 978-1910924-95-2
Ebook ISBN: 978-1-910924-86-0

Acknowledgments

This book and its author owe a debt of gratitude to numerous comrades scattered across the globe. My thinking about politics, economics, and cinematic horror has been shaped by ongoing and intermittent conversation – sometimes combative, always enjoyable – with Sam Dickson, Rory Dufficy, Grace Hellyer, Alexander Howard, Ruth Jennison, Angelos Koutsourakis, George Kouvaros, and Julian Murphet. Alex and Ruth both read drafts of the manuscript, and their suggestions improved it tenfold. The team at Repeater are on the right side of history. Thanks there to Mark Fisher for putting faith in this book when it was still an idea, Tariq Goddard who signed off on that idea and later provided editorial interventions, Josh Turner for the incisive copyediting, and Phoebe Colley for exterminating my numerous typos. The composition of this book coincided with the first year of my son's life, and many of the films discussed herein were watched and re-watched with him asleep on my chest. The existence of this book is therefore due in a very material sense to Finn Montague, who for so long refused to sleep on anything besides his parents and thereby ensured lengthy stretches of time with little else to do but sit and think before a glowing screen. A thousand thanks are due to Kate Montague, without whose intelligence, patience, and generosity this book would never have existed. Kate gives me reason to be. And, finally, this book is dedicated to my grandmother, Doreen Arahill, who not only allowed me to rent all sorts of horrific films when I was much too young to do so on my own, but who also watched them with me.

Table of Contents

The radical and mechanical separation of the concepts of violence and economics could only arise at all because... the fetish of the pure objectivity of economic relations obscures the fact that they are really relations between men and so transforms them into a second nature which envelops man with its fatalistic laws.
Georg Lukács

And then, above all, there is the new arrival – the thinking that does not shy away from the horror of the world, the darkness, but looks it straight in the face, and thus passes over into a different kingdom, which is not the kingdom of darkness.
Henri Lefebvre

GOT ME A MOVIE AH HA HA HO
SLICIN UP EYEBALLS AH HA HA HO
The Pixies

Chapter One

Introduction

Capitalism: A Horror Story

A bizarrely sweaty and visibly troubled man stands before a red backdrop. He has that look about him. The one preceded by an unconscionable ordeal. Some would call it the thousand-yard-stare. He reads a memorandum in deadpan, all slow and shaky, without looking directly into the camera:

> This picture, truly one of the most unusual ever filmed, contains scenes which under no circumstances should be viewed by anyone with a heart condition or anyone who is easily upset. We urgently recommend that if you are such a person or the parent of a young or impressionable child now in attendance that you and the child leave the auditorium.

These words are delivered as the epigraph to Michael Moore's 2009 documentary about the global financial crisis, *Capitalism: A Love Story*. Their recitation gives way to Iggy Pop's anthem for post-socialist, anti-capitalist discord, a swaggering rendition of "Louie Louie," used here to soundtrack CCTV footage of numerous bank stick-ups. "The communist world is falling apart," drawls the aging rocker, "the capitalists are just breaking hearts." Balaclavas, baseball bats, and backpacks full of cash. Despite its apparent irony, there's an irrepressible exuberance to this. Here bank robbery looks as fun as it is heroic. But is this, a gleeful pageant of armed insurrection, what those with heart conditions and the easily upset and young or impressionable children should avoid? No. Such an exhilarating assemblage of sound and image is not the picture against which this sweaty, troubled man had hoped to caution us.

The warning is lifted from archival footage. It originates in the coming attraction announcement for the first ever splatter film, *Blood Feast*, directed by Herschell Gordon Lewis and released in 1963. There and then it served as more of a come-on than a genuine caution, and in this capacity the two recitations are similar, but that is where the similarities appear to end. In its original iteration it challenged heedless cinemagoers to weather out a very different montage. What followed was a barrage of shots in which tongues and hearts and scalps and limbs are all amputated from their bodies without much in the way of narrative context. Nothing like a socially conscientious documentary, this was gratuitousness of a higher order, a bloody mess the likes of which had never before hit the celluloid. Its goal was to galvanize an audience through reverse psychology. "We figured," Lewis would later reflect, "if that didn't keep them in their seats nothing would."[1]

I begin here not only to telegraph the variously grotesque and consistently gruesome films on which this book fixates – consider this a half-facetious caution for the sensitive reader and a playful bait for the intrepid – but also because the warning's recurrence after almost half a century intimates a potentially meaningful relationship between cinematic gore and economic crises. Between spectacles of mutilation on the one hand, and the determinations of a failing economy on the other. Between splatter and capitalism. That relationship is the focus of this book, the task for which is to show how a popular sub-genre of horror cinema lays claim to a uniquely critical perspective on our historical situation. "Luridly," we have been told, "the horror of the ending lights up the deception of the origin."[2] That was the most stolid of all thinkers, Theodor Adorno, describing the function of serious art in 1951. But what he was saying then is doubly true of splatter now, one of the most lurid forms of art to occupy the dizzying onrush of a world-historic ending. That is to say, we have reached a moment in time when the seemingly invincible machinery of capitalist accumulation must once again rezone and reassemble, and yet such a process seems increasingly doubtful given the world-system's material limits. It is this imminent ending, the fatal haemorrhage of capitalist value, to which splatter responds.

According to Siegfried Kracauer, writing in his psychological history of German cinema during the rise of Nazism, "films address themselves, and appeal, to the anonymous multitude. Popular films – or to be more precise, popular screen motifs – can therefore be supposed to satisfy existing mass desires."[3] Yes, of course they do, but what desire is being satisfied by splatter? My theory is this: splatter, with its screen motifs of violence and gore, knows that when capital inscribes itself into our bodies and when our bodies are hardwired into capital what we are experiencing is a protracted mutilation whose internal processes are both accelerated and destabilized in times of crisis. Splatter confirms and redoubles our very worst fears. It reminds us of what capital is doing to all of us, all of the time – of how predators are consuming our life-substances; of how we are gravely vulnerable against the machinery of production and the matrices of exchange; and of how, as participants of an internecine conflict, our lives are always already precarious.

For reasons we will soon discover, the particular brand of horror mobilized in splatter is extremely responsive to the internal contradictions that threaten the future sustainability of capitalist accumulation. And, while responding to the prospect of that end with all the attendant shocks of global cataclysm, splatter nevertheless promotes an extant truth: capitalist accumulation is and always has been a nightmare of systematized bloodshed. This book provides an account of that nightmare as told through a combination of economic history, filmic analysis, and personal reflection. Its task is to sift through the shambles, exploring splatter for both its consistencies and its derivations, whose interplay might serve us as a source of theoretical and practical knowledge for surviving the horror movie we all collectively inhabit.

Mutilation is the Message

Splatter's defining gesture is to capture in loving detail the abject moment when human bodies are destroyed irreparably. Splatter invites us to wallow in the gore, and to take pleasure doing so. It wilfully gratifies our bloodlust. As a film genre, the stylistic signature of splatter is what Colin Milburn describes as the "representational moment in which the human body is violently torn asunder, shredded, sliced, hacked, dismembered, melted, and transformed, splattered as semiotic fluid into ghastly forms of monstrous abjection."[4] Or, as John McCarty has phrased it using a well-known alliteration, this is the one genre in which "mutilation is indeed the message – many times the only one."[5] While, for this reason, I use the terms "splatter" and "gore film" interchangeably, it must nevertheless be clarified that even though a film might contain scenes of gore, those scenes will not guarantee that it is indeed a splatter film.

First, splatter is a sub-genre of horror: it wants to elicit negative reactions from an audience, primarily by exploiting our primal fears. While Mel Gibson's Jesus movie, the fourth Rambo flick, and most of Quentin Tarantino's oeuvre are all exceedingly violent, their violence isn't designed to fire unpleasant cognitive processes; their violence is not the violence of horror, and so they are not splatter films. Second, when it comes to splatter, plot is equally important as the gore it frames – the plot or, more often than not, the plot's apparent deficiencies. Here narrative is chiefly a concocted means for transporting an audience from one scene of carnage to the next, thereby depicting gore as inevitable; not necessarily inescapable, but seemingly omnipresent. While this convention lends many of the films an incredibility more appropriate to slapstick comedy than to horror – and indeed, comedy frequently counterbalances genuine terror – it also suggests why splatter might have something to say about capitalism in its late, multinational, and global configuration, a mode of production whose outwardly absurd machinations barely conceal a structure that ensures a superabundance of violence. That, our fearful reaction to the mode of production, is precisely what splatter exploits in its convergence with horror.

But why might splatter films be as interested as they are in the seemingly extraneous machinations of the economy, and why might they then give their representation of those machinations a distinctly anti-capitalist spin? This book's focus on splatter as an emphatically popular genre means the films under consideration here attain heuristic value as privileged case studies for a very specific argument. To be sure, popular cinema has always been the recipient of a mediating code that forges links between film form and economic history. As Fredric Jameson once argued, popular cinema exemplarily manifests "that dimension of even the most degraded type of mass culture which remains implicitly, and no matter how faintly, negative and critical of the social order from which, as a product and a commodity, it springs."[6] Splatter films are popular, but they are simultaneously marginalized. Traditionally sustained by grindhouse theatres and cheaply produced videos, even since becoming more accessible splatter holds an outsider status, inassimilable into the mainstream. These films seem to recognize their status not only as commodities but also as an aggressive reaction against the marketization of particular images. Indeed, early splatter performed its marginalization from Hollywood in low-rent productions that would be an embarrassment to the well-funded studio system.

Reflecting this situation at the level of narrative, where those contextual matters and production issues can be expressed unambiguously, splatter films regularly concern themselves with violence enacted by the economically disenfranchised and the socially marginalized, and regularly against the beneficiaries of that system which ensures their status as underclass. If mutilation is indeed the message, here that message is delivered by immigrant shopkeepers, unemployed abattoir workers, and burnt-out scientists; by the tribal victims of colonial expansion, the immiserated masses of post-socialist shock doctrines, and the enslaved citizens of a prison-industrial complex; by the hillbilly opponents of a long-secured federation. Splatter's antagonistic subjectivity belongs to those whose exclusion from the commodity is at its uttermost brutal. The true heroes of splatter are the victims of capital.

Styles of Violence: Splat, Slash, Snuff

One of the well-grounded clichés about modern liberalism pertains to its stance of nonviolence; that it endorses a toothless progressivism and shuns any sort of armed struggle; that, from its standpoint, to resist oppression through violent means makes you an oppressor too. Splatter promotes the opposite worldview. It reminds us that capitalism is already violent, that under capitalism violence is ambient and systematic, and that capitalism will only yield through greater and different violence. In the words of usually nonviolent Rosa Luxemburg, here countering the ideal of leftist reformism: "the violence of the bourgeois counter-revolution must be opposed by the revolutionary violence of the proletariat."[7] This axiom could just as easily belong to any number of comparably martyred embodiments of anti-capitalist opposition, from Louis Auguste Blanqui through to Leon Trotsky, right down to Malcolm X.

While splatter's various iterations all privilege scenes of wanton bloodshed, and while splatter frames that bloodshed as horror, it will be illuminating to extricate it from at least two comparably violent and closely related styles of the horror genre from which it derives: the slasher film, whose commercial popularity peaked in the 1980s and which dominated the market well into the 1990s, and the more obscure excrescence known in some shadowy corners of the internet as extreme horror. Before that, however, I want to insist pre-emptively that these sub-generic distinctions are provisional. They should be taken for what they are, not as attempts to definitively theorize splatter or to posit yet another theory of genre, but as rough guidelines to help explain why this book is interested in some movies and not others. They also mean to indicate that there is something necessary to splatter's outstanding take on violence, something lacking in comparable forms, which makes it singularly apposite to the task at hand.

Unlike splatter, which exists almost solely for the violent act and its messy aftermath, the slasher film is more interested in the threat of violence and in sustaining that threat's dramatic tension. Slasher films are about the thrill of the chase. Splatter is about the joy of the kill. As a very basic rule of distinction, if a film relishes gore more than tension it is likely splatter, but if it enjoys tension more than gore it is likely a slasher. Though it might seem pedantic, this point of difference contributes to the slasher film's entrenchment within the conservative wing of cinematic horror.

What slasher films ultimately provide in the climactic terminations of their frequently coherent narratives is the dispersal of dramatic tension, and with that dispersal comes ideological closure and political containment. The sympathetic hero's inevitable victory over the agents of evil restores a social order, which is all too regularly white, middle-class, and suburban. That victory conjures away whatever antagonism might have been embodied in the promise of violence, even if only temporarily. While there are obvious exceptions, some of the best-known and genuinely great slasher films are almost painfully conventional in their adherence to such a formula. Indeed, this kind of social restoration is what we encounter in the (obviously gendered) triumphs of Laurie over Michael Myers, of Alice over Mrs Voorhees, of Nancy over Freddy Krueger, of Sidney over Ghostface, and so on and so forth *ad infinitum*. When coupled with violence that recurrently serves as puritanical vengeance (i.e. in slasher films, sex and drugs mean certain death), the narrative convention of resolving tension in favour of an established social order predisposes the slasher film to a political code that is nothing short of repressive, if not avowedly reactionary, but with the exception of its potentially radical narratives about gender. Splatter, despite its mostly unforgivable take on an assumed war of the sexes, depicts an amoral world of omnipresent violence and irresolvable contradiction. In short, its narratives are just so much sloppier. In its manifold returns of the repressed, splatter denies the consolations offered by slasher films.

If splatter is significantly less coherent than slasher films, its commercial popularity and aesthetic accessibility nevertheless distinguish it from extreme horror, which is perhaps less of a generic descriptor than a measure of shock value. That said, the films I am thinking of here are the ones that variously exploit the verisimilitude of mondo shockumentaries and simulated snuff in a quest to assail hitherto untouched taboos. One key difference is that, while extreme horror tends to privilege episodic depictions of anonymous slaughter, splatter still situates its gore within perfunctory narratives and makes at least some minimal attempt at character development. Another difference is in the staging of that slaughter. Splatter films stylize their gore in such ways that the otherwise credible special effects tend to come off as theatrically spectacular, self-consciously cinematic, and to some extent unreal. In splatter, the blood is too red, the flesh too soft, and bodies don't just puncture – they erupt, explode, and disaggregate. There is grim humour in the hyperbole. By contrast, extreme horror favours the ultra-realism of shaky hand-held cameras and a flat aesthetic that eschews any such spectacle.

That aesthetic is what we see, perhaps least obscurely, throughout the Guinea Pig series from Japan made during the late 1980s, and more recently in Fred Vogel's August Underground films or to a slightly lesser extent in Lucifer Valentine's Vomit Gore Trilogy. One of the weirder episodes in cinema history is testament to the realism of extreme horror. When in 1991 Charlie Sheen was shown an extreme horror film – in which a man dressed a samurai kidnaps, tortures, and dismembers a young woman – he reported it to the MIAA on suspicion that it was genuine snuff, and thereby triggered a full-scale FBI investigation into the film's production. Emanating from that realism, what makes extreme horror so radically different from splatter is tone: despite or even because of its obscene violence the splatter film delights in a borderline camp exuberance, the kind you cheer along to in a rowdy cinema or in a room of friends. Comparatively, splatter's extreme counterparts are routinely miserable in their self-serious bids for transgression: not to be watched at the cinema, or with company, but in the basement, alone.

While slasher films speak to a conservative desire for the strengthening of capitalist order, the blank realism and committed miserablism of extreme horror resigns itself to apolitical nihilism. Splatter is neither conservative nor apolitical. It is politically committed and its commitment tends toward the anti-capitalist left.

Q. What is Capitalism? A. The Moving Contradiction.

This book is unabashedly Marxist. One reason for this is that, as we are going to see in a subsequent chapter, Karl Marx styled his prose in such a way as to anticipate gore films and maybe even inaugurate pre-cinematic splatter. Another reason, which will be rehearsed here, is because Marxism and the Marxist theory of value provide an exceptionally rigorous framework for explaining both the social structures of capitalism and the reasons why capitalism must constantly face off against the crises to which splatter seems maximally responsive. Here I want to outline that theory and introduce the technical terms with which we will be describing capitalism.

This book thinks about capitalism as the dynamic interrelation between two conjoined levels of one economic system. Those levels will be viewed in close-up and as a long shot, to put it in filmic terms, and those two views will then be sequenced back together into the montage called history. Our close-up depicts capitalism as the transformation of living labour into surplus value. Within the wage relation, individual workers produce sellable commodities on behalf of the capitalist by whom they are employed. Value is generated when the worker is remunerated for less work than he or she put into the production of whatever commodities. That work, labour, is the one and only source of value. Surplus value is therefore born of labour's exploitation. Zooming out, our long shot depicts capitalism as a world-system articulating numerous sites of production into a single, global market. This articulation is what enables the exchange of value-larded commodities and thus an individual profit for the capitalist who sells them. Our close-up is of production, or manufacture, and our long shot is of exchange, or the market.

An illustration might help explain how this works, as well as introduce our remaining terms, namely fixed and variable capital. Imagine that you are the capitalist and I am the worker. You employ me with the task of producing, say, a chainsaw. You provide me with all of the raw materials – metal, plastic, motor parts, a chain – as well as the tools I need to assemble them. We call the raw materials and the tools utilized in production *fixed* capital, because they will cost you a fixed sum of money, and no matter what the circumstances they cannot make themselves more valuable. My labour, which you have also paid for, is called *variable* capital, because it can valorise those things. It can make them more valuable. Here's how. Say the fixed capital cost you $75. Now, say I charge $25 per hour for my labour, and it takes me one hour to make the chainsaw. I hand you the chainsaw, which as a new commodity has absorbed the cost of both fixed and variable capital, and you then take it off to market and sell it to a man in a butcher's apron who can only squeal and grunt. He pays you $150. The chainsaw's final value is realized in that price, out of which $100 covers your outgoing expenses – on both fixed and variable capital – while the other $50 is yours to keep. But, if the chainsaw is valued at $150, and if I have only been remunerated $25, then I the worker am short-changed by $50. That $50, the difference between how much you paid and how much you earn from my labour, is the realization in profit of what we call surplus value.

The relationship between our two levels, between production and exchange, ensures the survival of capitalism and of capitalist accumulation. Manufacture and the market need one another. However, the relationship is not one of harmony but of opposition. There is a fundamental incongruity between our close-up and our long shot, which presents itself when the two are sequenced together. While surplus value can only arise in production by way of living labour's exploitation, and while it is only subsequently transformed into an individual profit though commodity exchange, the competitive struggle for profit within the field of exchange urges the cutting of production costs and therefore the reduction of living labour within the production process.

Returning to our imaginary scenario, you find yourself in market competition, against another captain of the chainsaw industry, who is selling his hardware for $120 a piece, for $30 cheaper than what you are offering. He must have a more efficient worker. To remain competitive, you drop your price. But, having dropped your price, you realize you are no longer turning as significant a profit, and so you lower your own production costs. Fixed capital is fixed capital, which means you can't lower its cost. But variable capital can be made more productive. You task me, your worker, with producing more chainsaws and to produce them quicker. No more time for artisanal blade-work or for lunch breaks; the new quota is five saws per hour. I can't keep up – there's an accident, I saw off my own hand – and so you replace my tools with a machine, which does most of the work instead of me. The machine is costly, but you no longer need to supply my tools and my labour is barely needed anymore. "The instrument of labor," says Marx, "when it takes the form of a machine, immediately becomes a competitor of the workman himself."[8] I now come in only once a day and load up the machine with raw material, charging $25 a week, while the machine produces fifty chainsaws per day, two hundred and fifty per working week, which you then take to market and sell for $110 a piece, making less profit per chainsaw but, for you, things just about even out through the sale of multiple cheaply-produced chainsaws.

Sure, your worker lost a hand because of hazardously accelerated conditions of production, and sure, I am now barely employed and can no longer afford to sustain myself, but where is the real harm in this? By real harm, I mean harm to capitalism as a system. How does this effect capitalist accumulation on the whole? The machine with which you effectively replaced me is fixed capital. It cannot valorise. Now remember that living labour is the sole source of value and when its role is diminished so is the gap between the price of fixed capital and the price for which the commodity is sold on the market. And with that decrease in value eventually comes a decrease in individual profits. You are now only making $10 per chainsaw, and need to sell five to earn what you once made from one sale. The market has thus betrayed manufacture. Here value, the requisite for capitalist accumulation, is ultimately thwarted by a system that depends almost exclusively upon its wherewithal. This dynamic is what Marx called "the moving contradiction," a phenomenon which is dangerous for workers who are either made redundant or brutalized by an increasingly exploitative labour process, and which is also a threat to capitalist accumulation on the whole, because without new value there is nothing new to accumulate.[9] When capitalism ceases to accumulate we enter a crisis, industry shuts down, and workers suffer.

One of the principal means by which capitalism displaces the crises wrought by the moving contradiction is through finance, which is an attempt to extract profits from the field of exchange as opposed to production. When the declining returns in surplus value cause a fall in profits, it is finance that temporarily restores profitability. Having ceased to make a profit in the chainsaw industry, you decide to withdraw all funds from production and reinvest them into the market itself. You buy shares in the knife industry, which soon goes under in the same way that the chainsaw industry did, and then with the knife-producer you form an alliance and, keeping clear of production altogether because it is just not as profitable as it used to be, you invest in bonds, stocks, futures, and derivatives, and you start lending money at interest.

Production is nothing and exchange is everything. Profits abound. However, because finance does not source its profits in production, in labour, or in value, this resolution can only be temporary. Rather than a new source of value, finance is a struggle between capitalists over already existing profits and a speculative claim on future value. Labour still exists, naturally, but in other times and other places. The market becomes capitalism's only source of profit. "Turn and twist then as we may," writes Marx of finance, "the fact remains unaltered. If equivalents are exchanged, no surplus value results, and if non-equivalents are exchanged, still no surplus value. Circulation, or the exchange of commodities, begets no value."[10] Indeed, the finance sector's post-crisis assertion of pre-eminence over the economy as a whole comes at the cost of burying contradiction even deeper within itself. There is no new value to accumulate, only extant profits to rearrange. This cannot last. Expect more crises.

Splatter and Capital, Together in History

Historically, the moving contradiction manifests in the transference of capitalist accumulation from the geographic locale of one hegemonic superpower to the next. These hegemons have been the city-state of Genoa, the United

Provinces of the Dutch Republic, the British Empire, and the United States of America. China might be next. The transference from one hegemon to the following takes place through a series of crises. According to world-systems theorist Giovanni Arrighi, this geopolitical dimension of capitalism moves in cycles, and each cycle can be divided into three phases: first, a hegemon shores up its powers through expansion in production and manufacture, but with market competition this growth is inevitably threatened by the moving contradiction; then, a shift in profit extraction from production into finance constitutes the "signal crisis," masking that contradiction whilst further attenuating the creation of value and thereby forecasting an endpoint for the hegemon's cycle; and finally, the "terminal crisis," in which finance collapses because it wants for value, and with that collapse the formerly displaced contradiction in production returns with a vengeance, causing the dissolution of a hegemon.[11]

If, during Marx's time, capitalist hegemony found home in the British Empire's nation state, for us in the late twentieth and early twenty-first century it is still situated on American soil, where it has been since the 1940s. However, for at least half a century the American hegemon has been racked by contradiction and by crises both signal and terminal. Things are going to hell. Or, rather, things went to hell a long time ago, but we're only now noticing all the fire and the brimstone. In short, the American cycle cannot last much longer and, importantly for this book, the twin crises bringing that cycle to an end bracket the historical situation in and through which splatter emerged.

Splatter flooded mainstream cinema in two distinct waves, both of which coincide with and maybe even correspond to the crises in capitalism, or American capitalist accumulation, first signal and then terminal. The first wave of splatter peaked during the 1970s, and the second wave in the mid-to-late 2000s.

In the period from the 1960s through the 1980s, American hegemony faced off against its signal crisis, transforming its economy from one of production to one based in finance; it leapt out of manufacture and into the market. In response to a massive decline in profit – by 1970 the rate of industrial profit was down 20 percent on its highpoint in the 1960s – American capital embraced credit, speculation, and investment. The economists Leo Panitch and Sam Gindin explain this signal crisis in accumulation with some handy stats: "the amount of capital invested by non-financial corporations grew at the historically high rate of 4.3 percent (adjusted for inflation) per year between 1967 and 1973, compared with an average 3.1 percent over the years 1949-66."[12] The key word here is "invested," for on it rests the initial leap from industry into finance. While these investments were motivated by the collapsing rate of profit in manufacture, a result of the moving contradiction's diminishment of value, the transformed economy has more recently incurred another, terminal crisis. That crisis began in the seemingly dull sector of mortgage credit, where finance mediated working class access to housing, before spreading outward into the esoteric fields of interbank lending and commercial investment, and then coming down on the extant zones of manufacture and every other sector of society. From mid-2007 until the end of the following year, the whole economy went visibly into meltdown, with 3.3 million jobs vanishing from industry and with households losing $14 trillion (22 percent) of their net worth.

The first wave of splatter coincides with that initial turn, from manufacture to finance, and the second wave with the revelation that finance was not a new economy, but the temporary displacement of that first crisis through a different kind of profiteering. Two crises, signal and terminal, and two waves of splatter, then and now.

Moving beyond mere coincidence or argument by analogy, my intuition is that gore, the invariable ingredient for splatter, responds to the vicissitudes of value, the invariable condition for capitalist accumulation. Gore emphasizes the materiality of bodies and brains, of the human substance within an economy made seemingly abstract because it has become financial but which is nevertheless dependent upon labour as the sole source of value. If the recent crisis in capitalist accumulation gave us a situation in which the law of capitalist value reasserted itself with unforgiving clarity, it is in the consolidated context of crisis that the splatter film's economic perspicacity should attain to full intelligibility.

As we are going to see, splatter has an unforgiving clarity of its own. There is an important bifurcation to splatter's affective energy, one that ramifies the historical dialectic of reification and utopia that plays out in all of popular cinema. Arrighi has introduced several revisionist parentheses into Joseph Schumpeter's familiar description of capitalism as "creative destruction" to insist that, "before humanity chokes (or basks) in the dungeon (or paradise)" of a capitalist world order, it might well "burn up in the horrors (or glories)" of antagonism.[13] Splatter knows to sense crises, but it also knows to seize them as an opportunity and to mobilize an insurrectionary logic of its own design. Time and time again, splatter provides the fantasy scenarios in which we, the dispossessed and disenfranchised, seek our bloody reparations. No strangulation without exhilaration. No dungeon without paradise. No horror without glory.

And yet, this book's narrative arc is not one of revolution, liberation, or even resistance, or at least not increasingly so over time. Though my argument posits the end of capitalism, it does not point toward utopia. Rather, splatter's evolution through two economic crises and the intervallic period between them reflects the historical degradation of labour, which has been variously eradicated, atomized, outsourced, and offshored, all while the finance sector grows in strength and dominance. Accompanying the degradation of labour is a palpable diminution of insurrectionary potential. This is a tendency Steven Shaviro identifies as common to our own lived experience of the present, and to the media he describes as post-cinematic. "All impulses of desires," he writes, "all structures of feeling, and all forms of life, are drawn into the gravitational field, or captured by the strange attractor, of commodification and capital accumulation."[14] Splatter is both a product and a symptom of subsumption, by which I mean living labour's integration into the wage-commodity nexus and its subsequent reconstruction to meet the dictates of capital. It too is pulled into and transformed by that gravitational field. We know this because its tone shifts drastically over the course of roughly half a century, from a genre whose films relish bloody convulsions in the social machinery to a genre whose films helplessly explore a seemingly inescapable totality.

"You have nothing to lose but your chains," goes the old communist adage. Maybe. But in the second wave of splatter the exuberance that would otherwise attend such an imperative has drained to almost nothing, and one film even suggests that the only way to cast off the shackles is to saw through your own ankles. That is the fundamental difference between the first and the second waves of splatter, between then and now, and it is a difference we can ascribe to the historical foreclosure of political and economic alternatives, at least from the standpoint of the United States, and to the degradation of a cohesive working class under neoliberalism.

Précis of the Present Book

In which films does all of this obtain cogent expression? And what corollary form does my argument take for the subsequent chapters, which together narrate the historical unfurling of splatter and capitalism? The following pages alternate between long chapters and brief intermissions. The chapters, outlined below, account for the historical evolution of splatter, from its prehistory in the nineteenth and early twentieth centuries, through its popularization in the second half of the twentieth century, and as it evolved into body horror during the 1980s and then torture porn at the start of the twenty-first century. Between these chapters are intermissions, which speak to this book's firm grounding in biographical particulars.

It was Jean-Paul Sartre who, conjuring an image deeply redolent of splatter, once insisted that "Marxism ought to study real men in depth not dissolve them in a bath of sulphuric acid."[15] For some readers, this book's view of history will be overly schematic for the sake of conventional film studies, and perhaps it will even appear as a liquefaction of the horror film's true subjectivity. For several decades, the established theories of cinematic horror have all tended to explore the precious depths of individual experience, primarily scanning cinema for lessons in sexual identity and cultural trauma, and often doing so in ways that might seem distant from or incommensurable with a systemic theory of capitalist accumulation. With the intermissions, I bring the arguments of this book into conversation with some of that theory. I do so by reflecting on my own lifelong enthusiasm for a particular kind of horror film, on the origins of that enthusiasm in my childhood and adolescence, and on the VHS culture through which it was initially mediated. I also use these reflections as points of departure from which to introduce theoretical claims about splatter and about how to think splatter in terms of economics, doing so via the films through which the genre was introduced to me. Whereas the chapters are arranged along a historical arc, the intermissions hold to biographical chronology; their arrangement is governed by the order in which I saw a handful of films that all had some impact on my taste in movies and on my thinking about gore. If the chapters build their argument out of economic history and filmic analysis, the intermissions are pitched somewhere between nostalgia and theory.

Chapter 2, Horrorshow Marxism, takes off from where this introduction ends. It illustrates a critique of capitalism and demonstrates how that critique is more than just analogous to what goes on in splatter films. Specifically, it shows how Marxism was absorbed into splatter's literary and cinematic prehistory. The chapter argues that the economic analysis produced by Karl Marx in the middle decades of the nineteenth century contained the aesthetic seeds of the splatter film, which then found their way into cinema via the work of Soviet director Sergei Eisenstein. After reading excerpts from Marx together with some episodes from the gothic novel as exemplary of Victorian-era splatter, the chapter then looks closely at scenes of gore in the films and film theory of Eisenstein, as well as in the films of three subsequent Marxist directors: Jean-Luc Godard, Dušan Makavejev, and Pier Paolo Pasolini. While this chapter is potentially eccentric in its choice of avant-garde and outwardly communist cinema, its delivery has been calculated to prepare for the subsequent chapters and their focus on popular cinema by unearthing a politically charged prehistory that appears to have been retained by more recognizable splatter. What those subsequent chapters would like to account for is a shared aesthetic ideology taken from the obverse side of film production. Popular splatter knows just as well that it too is telling the story of capitalism.

Chapter 3, American Fleshfeast, is about the first wave of American splatter. It looks closely at three films each released roughly one decade apart, and views them in relation to the signal crisis – when American capitalism was ultimately forced out of manufacture and into finance. These films are *Blood Feast* from 1963, *The Texas Chain Saw Massacre* from 1974, and *Day of the Dead* from 1984. All three are deeply interested in the fate of living labour immediately before, during, and soon after that crisis. Moreover, all three enact a quasi-socialist reversal of class relations, wherein the proletariat extirpates and consumes its bourgeois adversary. In addition to establishing the formal conventions of popular splatter, this chapter is especially interested in the representation of cannibalism, and in the way that these films are not content with simply letting their working-class antagonists eat the bourgeoisie. Rather, and taking things a step further, they all seem to delight in scenarios when the rich are forced to feed upon the flesh of their class allies.

The fourth chapter, Uncontrollable Organs, begins with the premise that, after the signal crisis in capitalist accumulation and the first wave of splatter films, American cinema turned to other and more conservative formulations of horror. In particular, it turned to quasi-theological movies about ghosts, hauntings, and possessions, and then to middle-class and suburban slasher films. Nevertheless, splatter resurfaces across the globe and in different guises, the most prominent of which is body horror. This chapter focuses on three body horror films all produced in different countries, and thinks about these films in relation to the forthcoming triumph of capitalism and liberal democracy over state communism. These films are *Videodrome* from 1983, *Hellraiser* from 1987, and *Society* from 1989. While the previous chapter addressed the signal crisis and its impact on manufacture or production, this one takes on the cultural logic of neoliberalism, a term used to describe the modality of capitalism that took shape between signal and terminal crises, and which was ushered in primarily under the governance of Margaret Thatcher and Ronald Reagan. While neoliberalism is taken as a sign of capitalism's supposed victory, its foreclosure against political and economic alternatives, body horror provides us with a countervailing satire on the neoliberal ideals of a networked society and its individuated entrepreneurs.

Spectacular Torture, the fifth chapter, leaps into the twenty-first century, where it thinks about the resurgence of gore, that second wave of splatter's popularity, in relation to the terminal crisis. It argues that if splatter's first wave reflected a signal crisis that primarily affected manufacture, and if body horror responded to the ascent of neoliberalism during the intervallic period between crises, the second wave responds to a crisis in financial circulation. The films that coincide with the terminal crisis are not just splatter but a new kind of splatter—less fun, more sadistic, but consistently popular and consistently anti-capitalist. They have been referred to as "torture porn." This chapter looks not at three individual films but at three series in which a single narrative is stretched out across multiple releases. These are the two *Hostel* films directed by Eli Roth in 2005 and 2007, the seven-film *Saw* franchise released between 2004 and 2010, and the *Human Centipede* trilogy, whose films were released in 2009, 2011, and 2015. Not only do these films thematize the new imperialisms of an apparently circulation-based economy, i.e. one of finance, they also enact that economy's structures at the level of their form. In short, the chosen examples of torture porn are all interested in the way that horrific images might distance themselves from the violent act itself—a dislocation that corresponds to the circulation of profits with little regard for production or for value—but they also collapse that distance, folding imagery and violence, finance and production, back into the one self-same and utterly grotesque form. Theirs is the horror of the always unchanging.

First Intermission
Nasty Videos

A confession: no matter what justifications I try to give it, the decision to write a book about splatter is, perhaps more than anything else, the result of my own puerile taste in movies. That taste seems to have been shaped by prolonged exposure to the genre during a potentially misspent adolescence in peri-urban nowhere on the east coast of Australia. To have started watching movies there in the mid-1990s, years before access to the internet, meant my first encounters with horror were all mediated by video rental stores – and, specifically, by floor-to-ceiling shelves of heroically sensationalist box art. This is how I first gained access to all sorts of visual atrocity, provided it could find commercial distribution in the wake of restrictions brought on by the so-called "video nasties" spat in England and against Australia's lastingly draconian system of film classification.

As a valiant surveyor of the aisles I was drawn to the very worst of whatever was on offer: namely, splatter, which was part of a horror section that always seemed to occupy the same space as porn. The marketing for these films, many of which barely made it through the censors unscathed, mined a similar affect to the trailer with which this book began, throwing down a challenge for the dumb and daring. With a truly demented cover image, a catchy tagline, a triptych of screenshots, and some snappy copywriting, the box art alone would fuel the imagination of movies infinitely more horrendous than anything that was available at the time. The films themselves consistently turned out to be the ugly assemblage of these representative part-objects, awkward in the intercalation of their own marketing materials, which we can only presume came after and not before the realized film.

Of all the videos I encountered during this time, the one that really sticks is *Blood Sucking Freaks*. This minor classic was released cinematically in 1976, right at the zenith of splatter's commercial popularity, but under an alternate title, *The Incredible Torture Show*, which replaced the even more colourful shooting title, *Sardu: Master of the Screaming Virgins. Blood Sucking Freaks* was retitled as such and reissued for video in 1980, and that is how I first encountered it, years later in 1998, and for better or for worse as an eleven year-old. The cover design was especially effective in establishing an aura of perversity that only found material buttress in the griminess of the box itself, an object I could only assume had been witness to all manner of local horror. I found myself haunted by that kind of thinking. "Just what kind of person would have rented this thing before me?" There was something inexplicably talismanic about it. A sacred artefact.

In an arch window coloured deep red against a black border and beneath the distributor logo was a composite image, little of which is taken from the film it promotes. A man in a suit, with his skull split down the middle, embraces a bikini-clad woman. The two are posed beside a silver calash being lifted to reveal a severed, bespectacled head. The word "FREAKS" in the film's title appears to be oozing blood. At the image's upper left corner was an official-looking and promissory warning: "This film contains scenes of a gross, disgusting nature and will offend." On the reverse side is the blurb text, which appears to misquote its own title: "They kill people for fun, they kill them slowly. They torture them, gouge their eyes out, suck their brains out... for fun. They are the BLOODSUCKING FREAKS." Beneath this are four screenshots: a dwarf grinning at an eviscerated eyeball; a man dressed in a white lab-coat drinking from an open skull through a long straw; another man's frenzied snarl; and another's face as he spits blood sideways across hanging chains. Before seeing the film, its artwork made perfectly clear that this would be an awesomely sordid experience. Game on, I thought.

Set in pre-gentrified Soho, Manhattan, *Blood Sucking Freaks* is about a Grand Guignol theatre run by master of ceremonies, Sardu, his dwarf assistant, Ralphus, and an unnamed dominatrix, who together torture and dismember women in front of paying audiences, as well as offstage for their own amusement. While the audience enjoys the carnage as little more than theatrical wizardry, the gore is indeed real, and the uniformly female victims have all been kidnapped, confined to cages, forced into cannibalism, and are either sold into slavery or murdered onstage. The plot focuses on the production of Sardu's theatrical opus, an avant-garde performance in which the abducted prima ballerina, Natasha Di Natalie, is brainwashed into kicking the teeth out of a theatre critic, Creasy Silo, who publically dismissed an earlier routine at the theatre as a "third-rate magic show."

When I first sat through this film it was easily the nastiest thing I had ever seen, with its overwhelming variety of violent acts, or what Sardu's namesake the Marquis de Sade would have called the criminal and the murderous passions: eyes are gouged, teeth pulled, limbs hacked; scenes of electrocution, medieval torture, and a guillotine beheading; loads of flesh-eating; necrophilia, which is played mostly for laughs; and, finally, a culminating scene that features the affectionate close-up on Sardu's severed penis, which has somehow found its way onto a hotdog bun with lettuce and which is being passed around between liberated slave-women. All of this was made even more memorable by what then seemed to me a unique aesthetic: the scenes are poorly lit, the soundtrack is functionally mono-instrumental, the acting worse than deplorable, the special effects thoroughly unbelievable, and the plot rudimentary at best. These apparent deficiencies only helped the film sear itself deep into memory by allowing a low-rent sleaziness to infect every aspect of the production, to shape its visual style no less than its explicit content. In the words of one particularly vivid though typically hostile review, which without a hint of irony recreates Silo's dismissal of Sardu's theatre: "When people use the term 'bottom of the barrel,' they often forget about the UNDERSIDE of the barrel, which is where poorly-made dreck like this belongs."[16]

Unforgettable though *Blood Sucking Freaks* might have been as my superlatively revolting introduction to splatter, what escaped me on that first encounter and until recently is the film's almost profound awareness of its historical moment and of that moment's economic structuration. In those rare episodes not preoccupied with sex and death or a heady combination of the two, dialogue refers us back to events particular to the United States, and especially to New York during the mid-1970s. This was a time when, faced with a national if not global crisis in capitalist accumulation, the city administration sought to avoid bankruptcy by butchering municipal and public services.[17] The corrupt NYPD officer hired to investigate Sardu reflects openly on his willingness to accept bribes, claiming that his father, another public servant, was recently made destitute after the state revoked his pension.

Sardu, by contrast, is portrayed as the entrepreneur, whose crimes are as motivated by class aspiration as they are by psychosexual sadism: his investment in the theatre is precisely that, a financial investment, which derives from a belief that just one successful production will enable his advancement from Soho to Broadway and then from Broadway to Hollywood. And while the nationwide economic crisis affecting New York was worsened by an oil embargo from the Middle East, Sardu opportunistically profits from precisely that oil shock, selling American women back to a Middle Eastern tycoon. "At last I'm glad to see some of the petrol dollars flowing back in this direction," Sardu opens their exchange. "I can't say I'm not doing my bit for the economy."

It is here that personal experience merges with film theory to produce a lesson about ideological criticism more generally. Recall Fredric Jameson's stipulation for the interpretation of popular film, his insistence that "genuine social and historical content must be first tapped and given some initial expression if it is subsequently to be the object of successful manipulation and containment."[18] That is precisely what we are hearing in this unmistakably referential dialogue – the tapping into and the initial expression of social and historical content, which the film then submits to ideological manipulation via narrative. This content is what I missed as an eleven year-old, but which now registers in such a way as to thoroughly transform the film's significance.

Honing in on those circumstantial details, we can confirm that Sardu's theatre is a fully-fledged business. Ralphus and the dominatrix are floor managers and the enslaved women serve as unpaid labour, advertised to the public as voluntary actors, or interns, for whom Sardu takes up a charity collection after each performance. "I smell money," announces the police officer on first entering the theatre, speculating on the necessity of further investigation not from the homicide department but from the IRS. "I always thought these off-off-Broadway gimmicks were a front for something else." While murder is the theatre's open secret, the film's barely less concealed truth is that its murders are all part of the sordid life of a capitalist during an economic crisis. But this isn't the real ideological payoff.

If it is true that popular cinema manifests an implicit criticism of the social order from which it emerges, and that as a marginal genre splatter might redouble such a criticism, the resultantly affirmative and anti-capitalist bent is exactly what we encounter at the conclusion of *Blood Sucking Freaks*. The tightly framed dick-in-a-bun is not just served up as one final gross-out, to elicit one last scream from the audience, but to concretize the film's utopian fantasy and to simultaneously ground that fantasy in the film's most primal horror. The slave's revolt with which this film ends and that culminating image together form a kind of insurgent barbarism: at long last, the capitalist has been murdered, beheaded, castrated, and eaten by his exploited workers. My introduction to splatter meant cheering along with morbid enthusiasm as the expropriator is well and truly expropriated.

Chapter Two

Horrorshow Marxism

The Slaughter-Bench of History

In 1916, approximately one year before the Russian Revolution, Vladimir Lenin reasoned for the unspeakable bloodbath that would almost certainly result from an armed insurrection. His justification for probable carnage reframed it as a revolutionary necessity, whose exceptional status would distinguish it from the omnipresent violence inherent to the incumbent mode of production. "Capitalist society," he maintained, "is and has always been horror without end."[19] The horror of which Lenin speaks here is focalized by that inter-imperialist struggle which had just arrived at its own grizzly and globalized apotheosis in the form of World War I. But horror also emanates from the fact of a readily perceptible endlessness: from our realization that, without forceful intervention against the system of capitalist accumulation, humankind will be subject everlastingly to the extraction of value via industrial torture.

History teaches us that Lenin and the Bolsheviks ultimately failed to dispose of their adversary's undead corpse, which continued to stalk the earth post-1917, and so Lenin's diagnosis has remained agonizingly true of things. For instance, it was in these posthumous words that Theodor Adorno looked back on the culture Lenin once sought to annihilate: "If one were drafting an ontology in accordance with the basic state of facts, of the facts whose repetition makes their state invariant, such an ontology would be pure horror."[20] Even though capitalism would continue to grow and mutate, to expand its reach and accelerate its internal processes, it would always do so in coherence with the diagnosis of ceaseless horror.

The strategies with which capitalism overcomes its

challenges, how it displaces its crises, are also horrific. This too has been articulated clearly enough. When describing capitalism's structural transmutation into its late or postmodern phase during the post-1970s effort to restore profitability through finance, Fredric Jameson finds it essential to pause his analysis and "remind the reader of the obvious," that even in this moment of ostensibly peaceful economic evolution, "as throughout class history, the underside of culture is blood, torture, death, and terror."[21] For Jameson, like Lenin and Adorno whom he echoes, horror obtains within the individual experience of capitalism, but it also provides the generic form of capitalism's world-historical invariability. And that systemic cycle, an ongoing repetition of crisis and resolution, conditions our experience of the historical present and haunts our visions of the future.

Crisis and resolution. Crisis and resolution. Crisis. Resolution. On it goes *ad nauseum*.

> Conjure, if you will, a primal sequence encountered in B-grade horror films, where the celluloid protagonist suffers a terrifying encounter with doom, yet on the cusp of disaster abruptly wakes to a different world, which initially seems normal, but eventually is revealed to be a second nightmare more ghastly than the first.[22]

This fittingly cinematic scenario, invoked by Philip Mirowski as the first sentence of his book about economic crises and their recuperation back into a neoliberal economy, is an arrestingly unsettled endpoint to this brief and incomplete lineage of Marxist thought, all of which screams out at the horrors of capitalism. Like the seemingly omnipotent franchise killers, capitalism is not just unstoppably horrific. It horrifies in its apparent unstoppability.

How, then, might we orient ourselves within a social dynamic whose very essence is horror? One answer, which will be pursued in the following pages, is to embrace a decidedly literal permutation of those critical descriptions, observing what happens when anti-capitalist critique inspires a concomitant aesthetic program: when a critique of horror produces horrific forms. It is from inside such an aesthetic that we can begin thinking about our place in things. With this chapter I want to show that history's sharpest critique of capitalism, namely the communist science of dialectical materialism, ultimately cultivated the aesthetic ideology of splatter. I want to show how the types of figuration first mobilized by Karl Marx in the middle of the nineteenth century were later taken up by the Soviet filmmaker Sergei Eisenstein. I then want to show how Marx and Eisenstein cast a shadow over film history in such a way that the horrors they describe and visualize reoccur in both communist cinema and in popular splatter. While subsequent chapters will show how popular films retain traces of this prehistory, a closer look at Marxism as its own singularly critical manifestation of splatter will help us polish a lens through which to project our vision of the historical period when splatter films rose to prominence. So, back to where it all began.

Gothic, Gore, *Gallerte*

Cinema is by no means the first medium to respond to capitalism as a source of horror or to engage it via an aesthetic of splatter. Horror fiction underwent multiple permutations throughout the eighteenth and nineteenth centuries and especially during the first industrial revolution, when it solidified generically into the gothic. It was in this period – during which all feudalistic and non-capitalist social structures were obliterated; when human bodies became increasingly subject to market forces; and when new hierarchies of dominance and subordination hardened – that we find the origins of modern horror, and with those origins we encounter the prehistory of splatter. All of this is readily discernible if we read Mary Shelley's *Frankenstein* from 1818 and Bram Stoker's *Dracula* from 1879, two books in which literary horror responds to the traumatic experience of early-industrial capitalism.

Though similar claims could be made about other gothic writings – think of the magnificent Edgar Allan Poe writing contemporaneously from across the split – here we will follow the lead of literary critic Franco Moretti, for whom these two books should be read together and as one. These books are mutually beholden because their central figures, the monster and the vampire, embody the dialectical antipodes of one divided society:

> They are indivisible, because complementary, figures; the two horrible faces of a single society, its *extremes*: the disfigured wretch and the ruthless proprietor. The worker and capital: 'the whole of society must split into the two classes of *property owners* and propertyless *workers*.' That 'must', which for Marx is a scientific prediction of the future (and the guarantee of a future reordering of society), is a forewarning of the end for nineteenth-century bourgeois culture.[23]

Frankenstein's nameless monster is literally stitched together from deceased members of a blighted underclass. He is an embodiment of the proletariat, the ungodly collectivization of otherwise disaggregated subjects into a single, productive, and altogether menacing entity. Dracula, inversely, is less the feudal aristocrat that his title might imply than he is a monopoly capitalist, whose migration from Transylvania to London is one of imperial expansion. His estate agent, Jonathan Harker, is acutely aware of what Dracula stands for. "This," diarizes Harker, "was the being I was helping to transfer to London, where, perhaps for centuries to come, he might, amongst its teeming millions, satiate his lust for blood, and create a new and ever-widening circle of semi-demons to batten on the helpless."[24] Vampire and monster, propertied and propertyless, bourgeoisie and dispossessed: the two poles of capitalist society.

These two figures are obvious staples of gothic horror – but what about gore, the essential ingredient for splatter? That too is present in both of these novels, both of which lay it on thick and fast.

In *Frankenstein*, the monster's animation – or, rather, the combined reanimation of its various organs – only takes place after the eponymous narrator has, in graphic detail, accounted for the effect of death on human anatomy. "I saw," we are told, "how the fine form of man was degraded and wasted; I beheld the corruption of death succeed to the blooming cheek of life; I saw how the worm inherited the wonders of the eye and brain."[25] This excessively lavish account of the body's irreversible mortification, its repulsive decay, is retained into the living monster's anatomy, which is constructed via "secret toil" in "the unhallowed damps of the grave," and furnished by materials from the "dissecting room and the slaughter-house."[26] Here is Doctor Frankenstein's description of his creation:

> How can I describe my emotions at this catastrophe, or how delineate the wretch whom with such infinite pains and care I had endeavoured to form? His limbs were in proportion, and I had selected his features as beautiful. Beautiful! – Great God! His yellow skin scarcely covered the work of muscles and arteries beneath; his hair was of a lustrous black, and flowing; his teeth of a pearly whiteness; but these luxuriances only formed a more horrid contrast with his watery eyes, that seemed almost of the same colour as the dun-white sockets in which they were set, his shrivelled complexion and straight black lips.[27]

Beauty is betrayed by horror. Perfect proportion gives way to a bloody, rotten mess. Enlightenment rationality meets its obverse in the death's head. The bourgeois grave robber's crimes are inflicted, in this first instance of Promethean creation, on the bodies of a working underclass which he has mutilated and reassembled, and which punctually turns against him in its own bloody quest for vengeance.

Similarly allegorical things can be said of the vampire and his insatiable thirst for human blood. Whereas *Frankenstein* reeks of death and decay, *Dracula* pulsates with plasmatic ichor, a material substance that surges through so many of the book's sentences as both a literary figure and a conditioning presence. Though in this novel blood is first a sign of human vitality, a cherished thing to be guarded at all costs, there is always either way too much or way too little of it, and in that scalar variance we encounter the book's unique sense of horror. The satiated vampire, for instance, appears as "gorged with blood" and swollen up "like a filthy leech."[28] Or, when a stake is put to the heart of one of Dracula's victims, the demon-possessed Lucy, she bites through her own lips until "the mouth was smeared with a crimson foam," and then comes the one true death: "driving deeper and deeper the mercy-bearing stake, whilst the blood from the pierced heart welled and spurted up around it."[29] That all of this blood belongs not to the vampire but has been expropriated from his victims is made plain when, in the final chapter, we are presented with a scene that should be as gruesome as Lucy's death, but instead shifts tone significantly, from bloody horror to bloodless supernaturalism:

> But on the instant, came the sweep and flash of Jonathan's great knife. I shrieked as I saw it shear through the throat. Whilst at the same moment Mr. Morris's bowie knife plunged into the heart. It was like a miracle, but before our very eyes, and almost in the drawing of a breath, the whole body crumbled into dust and passed from our sight.[30]

Without living bodies on which to feed the vampire is nothing but metaphysical ether.

It is no secret that Karl Marx more than just dabbled in writing this kind of horror. "Part of the genuine radicalism of Marx's critical theory," argues David McNally, "resides in its insistence on tracking and naming the monsters of modernity."[31] Indeed, Marx's writing overflows with tropes and figures born of the gothic. "Capital," we are told, "is dead labour, that, vampire-like, only lives by sucking living labour, and lives the more, the more labour it sucks."[32] Or, in the more complex (though awkwardly translated) formulation of valorisation:

> By turning his money into commodities that serve as the material elements of a new product, and as factors in the labour-process, by incorporating living labour with their dead substance, the capitalist at the same time converts value, i.e., past, materialised, and dead labour into capital, into value big with value, a live monster that is fruitful and multiplies."[33]

In these two sentences, both taken from the only published book that Marx himself brought to completion, potentially antiseptic accounts of economic procedures cleave the same tropology utilized by Stoker and Shelley, summoning predatory vampires and undead monsters. These figures are not just confined to the nineteenth century view of capitalism either. See, for instance, Chris Harman's book on zombie capitalism, in which the monster and the vampire have both lived on into the twenty-first century, enjoying an immortality tethered to the mode of production. "The runaway world," he says, "is the economic system as Marx described it, the Frankenstein's monster that has escaped from human control; the vampire that saps the lifeblood of the living bodies it feeds off."[34]

But Marx's account is not only gothic. His descriptions of a blood-drenched and gore-caked mode of production are even more prescient of splatter as we see it in recent cinema than were the writings of his novelist contemporaries. Where it lacks in their sense of morality it makes up for in cold rationality. His horrors are irredeemable and absolute. When Marx insists that capitalism is the mode of production that "comes dripping from head to foot, from every pore, with blood and dirt," he really commits himself, as a gifted writer and a master-stylist, to conveying specifically that kind of horror.[35] He does so by allowing his prose to modulate from the gothic into splatter.

Later, when the vampire image returns, narrative emphasis shifts from the bourgeois predator to the exploited worker, and specifically to the worker's obliterated body:

> It must be acknowledged that our labourer comes out of the process of production other than he entered. In the market he stood as owner of the commodity 'labour-power' face to face with other owners of commodities, dealer against dealer. The contract by which he sold to the capitalist his labour-power proved, so to say, in black and white that he disposed of himself freely. The bargain concluded, it is discovered that he was no 'free agent,' that the time for which he is free to sell his labour-power is the time for which he is forced to sell it, that in fact the vampire will not lose its hold on him 'so long as there is a muscle, a nerve, a drop of blood to be exploited.'[36]

The vampire reveals itself only when it is already too late, when the façade of legal niceties turns out to be an evil, Faustian pact, inescapable until the death of either party. Stylistically important is that quoted material at the end, taken from a description made elsewhere by Friedrich Engels. The quotation from Engels confirms the organic substance of capital, its own expropriated lifeblood, is the insides of the worker. The vampire feasts on those muscles, nerves, and blood. While Marx frequently draws on the patently gothic imagery of vampires, werewolves, and spectres, here we can see that his accounts of capital also acquire a taste for human viscera, with sentences chewing their way through bodily gristle.

Take, for another example, Marx's description of wage-labour as the industrial ingestion of human bodies. "The capital given in exchange for labour-power," he writes, "is converted into necessaries, by the consumption of which the muscles, nerves, bones, and brains of existing labourers are reproduced, and new labourers are begotten."[37] Born into capital we are not human subjects. We are only our capacity to work, which results from the utilization of our variously muscular and cerebral organs. If labour is the one source of value in capitalism, and if value therefore results from the consumption of our organic matter, then capitalism begins to look a whole lot like its own splatter film. Its grotesque substance, made up of muscles, nerves, bones, and brains, is the sinewy material of production, the very fundament of value, which is torn from its embodying labourers and fed into industrial machinery.

Capitalist accumulation is, as Marx knows, a crime whose most obvious analogue is cannibalism:

> We may say that surplus value rests on a natural basis, but this is permissible only in the very general sense, that there is no natural obstacle absolutely preventing one man from disburdening himself of the labour requisite for his own existence, and burdening another with it, any more, for instance, than unconquerable natural obstacles prevent one man from eating the flesh of another.[38]

In Marx's view, gore is the nurturing substance of value, and therefore of accumulation in general. Capitalism is Victorian-era splatter.

Descriptions like these were not written simply to lend

stylistic trimming. Rather, they get to the very essence of life under capitalism. They remind us how bodies and brains are mutilated into commodities. Recall that capitalism is a moving contradiction: that market competition encourages the reduction of labour time to a minimum while simultaneously positing labour power as the sole source of value. In this structural sense, which encourages the destructive pressurization of human labour by the acceleration of production, capitalism is both literally and figuratively the protracted splattering of human bodies. Literally, we need only think of the deformations, injuries, and fatalities caused by strained working conditions at every level of capitalist industry, from neurological trauma through to heart attacks, right down to broken bones, amputated limbs, and mass deaths. Figuratively, every minute and every hour spent in wage labour is another minute and another hour in which our bodies are wired to a vast machine that only lives by draining our life substances.

While the moving contradiction is a principal source of economic crises, the social relation it underwrites is what attracts Marx's most gruesome imagery. And, because the human carriers of labour power must also consume the commodities they have produced and valorised, capitalism also means unavoidably participating in the consumption of oneself and one's fellow workers. In short, capitalism is the grossest, most horrific splatter film you will ever see.

Here, finally, all of this boils down into a single figure. Into an unusual commodity that is both the literal and the figurative embodiment of life under capitalism. In a forceful re-reading of Marx focused on the question of disgust, poet and literary critic Keston Sutherland has recovered a core ontological concept, a figure that had been lost in translation out of Marx's German and into English. As Sutherland explains it, Marx never wrote that the commodity is made up of what Marx's translators refer to as "a mere congelation of homogenous human labour." The problem with words like "congelation" here and "frozen" elsewhere is that, as chemical processes, they are both remarkably sanitary and entirely reversible. This generates an ambiguity absent from Marx's original text. For Marx, labour's destination under capital is in what he calls "*Gallerte*," which "is now, as was when Marx used it, the name not of a process like freezing or coagulating but of a specific commodity," namely a comestible jelly made up of various animal parts cooked together into a grossly edible form: Soylent Green Pâté.[39]

Life under capitalism is the experience of *Gallerte*, the irreversible liquefying of human substance and its necrophagic consumption. Like the grim fate of the victims in any given splatter film, whose bodies are obliterated beyond all recognition and so frequently ingested by other humans, once labour succumbs to value that transformation is utterly irreparable. This is what Marx was trying to teach us all along with his own brand of splatter. In Sutherland's words: "All that is meat melts into bone, and vice versa; and no effort of scrutiny, will or heated imagination, however powerfully analytic or moral, is capable of reversing the industrial process of that deliquescence."[40] The lesson can be put this way: we all inhabit the same splatter film and we should all be intensely revolted by this. But, even if we cannot undo what has already been done, perhaps that revulsion will somehow lead to revolution.

Sergei Eisenstein: Godfather of Gore

We encounter this very deliquescence, the *Gallerte*, all throughout popular splatter films, but for the first time historically in 1925, with Sergei Eisenstein's *Battleship Potemkin*, when a maggot-infested borscht serves as catalyst for insurrection. However, it was another of Eisenstein's films that best captures labour's mortification as Marx described it, doing so in what I propose is cinema's first iteration of splatter. *Strike*, also from 1925, is about a factory-workers' revolt, triggered by fatally strenuous working conditions and then crushed by military force. The film's final reel, titled "Liquidation," depicts an armed assault on the striking factory-workers' tenements.

This reel includes what film critic David Bordwell describes as "the most abstract sequence of all," in which shots of a battalion firing rifles into a mass of fleeing workers are intercut with shots of a bull's disembowelment.[41] The first time the bull is struck, with a bolt to the skull, its fall is depicted from three different angles, before a medium shot depicts the approaching butcher in a long apron already slicked in blood. The next shots of the slaughter are all close-ups, in which we can see the whites of the animal's eyes. First an overhead shot onto the severing of its throat, sliced from top to bottom; the second retains the camera position of the first for the parting of that wound, with the butcher's assistant peeling open its oesophagus; the third, taken from a frontal low angle, shows the bull's head being twisted around, which causes its body and shoulders to spasm, ejecting another torrent of blood and gore. These images are interspersed within a scene that depicts the shooting of hundreds of anonymous workers. At the scene's end, when the eviscerated bull ceases to fight and its breath slows, we are presented with a long and slowly panning shot of the slaughtered workers. Their bodies line the same earth onto which we have seen the outpouring of animal blood.

The sequence is abstract, for Bordwell, because the images of the bull are entirely non-diegetic, included only to generate a cinematic metaphor that projects onto the workers' execution the overtones of industrial butchery. While the grammar of this montage is readily legible, what we see is so intensely affecting not for intellectual but for more basely physical reasons. The ultra-realist shots of the eviscerated bull arouse a horror that is transposed onto the murdered workers. Gore is used, in Eisenstein's words, to "stir the spectator to a state of pity and terror which would be unconsciously and automatically transferred to the shooting of the strikers."[42] In addition to reframing metaphorically the workers' deaths, this sequence taps into the same kind of horrific imagery Marx used to account for capitalist production. As it was with Marx, the goal here is revolutionary activation through bodily repulsion. In a word: *agit-guignol*.

Even though Eisenstein would later criticize this early film for having "floundered about in the flotsam of rank theatricality,"[43] earlier drafts of the script contained numerous other scenes that would have similarly presaged splatter, including one worker's dismemberment and another being liquefied in a cauldron of molten steel. Irrespective of directorial regrets, in this instance Eisenstein appears to us as both a student of Marx and cinema's true Godfather of Gore. The coincidence of these two things is by no means accidental.

This scene from *Strike* is not the first instance of gore to be captured on screen. Most notably, it postdates a handful of bloody shorts dedicated to historical slayings. These include Siegmund Lubin's *Beheading the Chinese Prisoner* from 1900 and Thomas Edison's *Execution of Mary, Queen of Scots* from 1905 – as well as the graphic impalement scene and decapitations from D.W. Griffith's *Intolerance* in 1916, and again in 1921 the torture of peasants and the guillotining of aristocrats from *Orphans of the Storm*. Though not entirely without precedent, *Strike* notably predates the scenes often cited as art-cinematic precursors to popular splatter: the ocular slicing from Luis Buñuel and Salvador Dalí's *Un Chien Andalou* in 1929; the slaughterhouse from Georges Franju's *Blood of the Beasts* in 1949 as well as the mutilations from his *Eyes Without a Face* in 1959; and the arterial-spray beheadings in Akira Kurosawa's *Sanjuro* in 1962.

But splatter is not just about special effects. It is not just about the fact of violence. It also depends on how that effect is framed and edited, on the formal and narrative emphasis of the violent act or its outcome. Indeed, when it comes to splatter we should pay close attention not only to the fact of gore, its mere presence on the screen or within the narrative, but also to what makes this gore unique, film-by-film, scene-by-scene, shot-by-shot. For that reason, we should at least gesture toward a more formalist argument on which to ground any claim to precedence, and insist that if Eisenstein's sequence does in fact inaugurate cinematic splatter, it does so through a transposition of material out of Marx's text not only into comparably violent content but also into some very specific filmic techniques. That is to say, Eisenstein gave splatter its form. But what exactly is that form?

In his notes toward a film adaptation of Marx's *Capital*, Eisenstein predicted that the adapted object would not be Marx's thematic content but, rather, dialectical materialism. "There are," he insists, "endlessly possible themes for filming in CAPITAL ('price', 'income', 'rent') – for us, the theme is Marx's method."[44] What we have seen in Eisenstein's *Strike* is the application of dialectical filmmaking, technically informed by Marx, to one of the themes about which Marx writes, namely class warfare. And, in the consonance between political content and politicized form, Eisenstein's film generated an exemplary instance of splatter. While Eisenstein famously adapted Marx's dialectical materialism for cinematic montage, the "Liquidation" from *Strike* is not just the combination of two otherwise disparate sequences into a visual metaphor, but also the combination of two kinds of shot: the long shot, for the multitude of anonymous workers, and the close-up, which emphasizes the violent act as it tears apart an individual body.

It is the non-diegetic images that constitute splatter, not only because of their bloody *mise-en-scène* but also because of how that *mise-en-scène* is framed in close-up or as what Eisenstein liked to call the "large-scale shot," positioning the viewer just inches from the open wound. This kind of shot is what Eisenstein also describes as a dominant form in his "montage of attractions," which is designed to stage the molecular irruption of sensual and psychological aggression, which for him finds inspiration in the theatrical equivalent to splatter. "Sensual and psychological, of course, are to be understood in the sense of immediate reality," he says, "in the way that these are handled, for example, by the Grand Guignol theatre: gouging out eyes or cutting off arms and legs on the stage..."[45]

In a different version of the same essay, and with specific reference to the close-up, Eisenstein describes how such a visual language would depict murder by associating individual "montage fragments," which together would form a cinematic totality: "a throat is gripped, eyes bulge, a knife is brandished, the victim closes his eyes, blood is splattered on a wall, the victim falls to the floor, a hand wipes off the knife – each fragment is chosen to 'provoke' associations."[46] While in Eisenstein's conception splatter finds precedent in the bloody verisimilitude of Grand Guignol, what makes cinema irreducibly different from that theatrical tradition is both its capacity to edit violent images into montage sequences, controlling the speed at which viewers engage with that content, and its capacity to bring the viewer closer than is feasible on the stage, primarily with close-ups. Montage and close-up: between the two splatter finds its language, a language autonomous to cinema, thereby attaining something more aesthetically radical than the mere staging of violent content.

Marxism Goes Grindhouse

If Eisenstein gave splatter its visual syntax by reworking Marx for cinema, subsequent directors also schooled in Marxism and evolving Eisenstein's lessons in filmmaking have continued to deal in gore using comparable techniques. Here we will look at three films that do this, the first of which is Jean-Luc Godard's *Weekend* from 1967. Godard's is an apocalyptic fable in which a *haut*-bourgeois couple, Roland and Corinne, conspire to murder one another whilst driving to Corrine's parents' home, where Corinne intends to secure an inheritance from her father and, if need be, murder him too. This film is, in Evan Calder Williams' estimation, "the brutal, illogical, and misanthropic burning wreck, breaking through not just that fantasy, but the very fantasy of capitalism's future persistence."[47] One of the ways this film serves as the fantasy-shattering vehicle for a Marxist critique of capitalism is by establishing a metaphorical link between cars and capital, presenting the automobile as a primary source of bourgeois accumulation and of reifying individualism, and by rethinking the roads, highways, and parking lots as a zone of class war turned Hobbesian clusterfuck. In short, Godard's film is about the inevitable and imminent crash of a largely Fordist industrial economy.

The film's most famous sequence comprises a lateral tracking shot whose slow movement barely outpaces the gridlock it depicts by keeping relatively close to Roland and Corinne's luxury convertible as it weaves opportunistically through stalled traffic. This long shot, which lasts for seven and a half minutes, takes us past numerous stalled cars, past just as many passengers disembarked onto the roadside, past a fleet of circus trucks with their animal cargo, past a horse and cart, past a garishly yellow Shell tanker with a small white car wedged head-on under its grill, past an elderly couple playing chess, past more cars, past a yacht with sails at full mast, and past yet more cars, all of which with its incessant honking ultimately introduces an image of horror: at the end of the road and causing the traffic jam a family has been killed in an automobile collision. Their bodies are torn to pieces and their blood is smeared and pooling all across the blacktop. A policeman directs traffic over shining slicks of dark-red gore. The three corpses, all mangled and contorted, have been dragged off of the road and are left on the grass in the shot's foreground. Roland and Corinne zoom ahead and take the first right. "See what happened to that Triumph?" asks Corinne in the next shot. "If only it were papa and mama." And yet, the cause of that traffic jam is only the first of several Ballard-esque atrocities to appear in the film. Later, a peasant crashes his tractor into a sports car, killing the male driver and spraying the female passenger in her lover's blood. Her protests swiftly turn from the deceased driver to the ruined car. "The heir to Robert factories gave it to me because I screwed with him."

The two grizzliest sequences in this film are both homages to Eisenstein's *Strike*, intercutting the murder of humans with animal butchery. The first is when Roland and Corrine finally arrive at her parents' chateau, but only after her father's slow death from poisoning, where they dispute Corrine's inheritance with her mother. Roland haggles down from a sixty-forty to a ninety-ten split, but is still told off on the grounds that, in such an arrangement, his mother-in-law would only receive $4 million. He rushes the old woman from behind, choking her with a scarf, and Corrine charges in with a butcher's knife. Cut to an extreme close-up on the face of a flayed rabbit, which is progressively doused in more and more blood. In the voiceover, Roland and Corrine discuss the body's disposal and their inheritance before declaring their love for one another.

Soon later, after their own foreseeable crash – "My Hermès handbag!" screams Corrine at the flaming wreckage and the piled corpses – the couple is kidnapped into a band of hippie revolutionaries and perverse cannibals, the Seine and Oise Liberation Front, whose radio call-sign is, of course, "Battleship Potemkin." Our second grizzly scene turns the violence back against Roland, when he tries to flee the Liberation Front and one of its members knocks him down with a slingshot. In the next shot Roland is framed from the chest up and with blood pooling around his head. "Why disembowel him?" asks Corrine. "It's best that way," responds one of his killers. We are then shown the group slaughtering animals in two coldly framed medium shots. First a pig's skull is cracked with a sledgehammer and its throat is opened up. Second a goose's head is roughly sliced from its still animate body. The flesh of Roland and of the animals, as well as "the leftovers of the English tourist," are combined and poached in a giant red drum, and are consumed as delicious. *Gallerte* redux. The film's lesson with its redoubling of gore on gore is, to quote one of the guerrillas: "The horror of the bourgeoisie can only be overcome by more horror."

Another example of Marxist-made splatter from the following decade, the 1970s, will help secure the historical overlap between this avant-garde and communist aesthetic and its more popular emergence. Dušan Makavejev's insanely perverted *Sweet Movie* from 1974 documents the horrors both of capitalist excess and of post-socialist corruption in the remnants of a statist ideology that ultimately failed to deliver the communist alternative. In Stanley Cavell's wonderful formulation, this is a film that "attempts to extract hope– to claim to divine life after birth–from the very fact that we are capable of genuine disgust at the world; that our revoltedness is the chance for a cleansing revulsion..."[48] To this end, *Sweet Movie* comprises two parallel stories: one is about a Canadian beauty queen whose hymen is declared champion of a virginity pageant and whose prize is marriage to a milk industry oligarch from America, and the other about a self-appointed sea captain commanding a boat through the canals of Amsterdam, to whose bow is affixed an enormous and shaggily bearded sculpture of Karl Marx.

These stories take every available opportunity to wallow in studiously psychoanalytic abjection, with the first story favouring sexual horror and the second something more akin to splatter. In that first story we are exposed to a fetishistic scene of weird pre-coital hygiene rituals, several shots of male urination, a prolonged instance of *penis captivus*, the apparent joys of adult breastfeeding, and a truly revolting episode of primal regression in which a grown man vomits and shits all over himself. Capitalism is presented here as the global expression of what Herbert Marcuse once called "repressive desublimation," a cultural logic in which the market administers sexual liberty as an instrument of political control.

While the first story's scabrous sense of humour is evidently attracted to episodes of sexual perversion, the second story, about the boat and its captain, includes more bloody horror of the type in which we are interested. The boat itself is little more than a floating appropriation of Soviet iconography, with its monumental images of Lenin and Trotsky and Stalin watching over its passengers' every move. That this story is in no way utopian or affirmative is signalled early on with an aside of black-and-white documentary footage showing the disinterment of corpses from the Katyn massacre in Poland, the largest mass execution undertaken on behalf of the Soviet Politburo and with Joseph Stalin's approval. In another scene, the ship's captain lures a band of dockside children aboard with the promise of candy, which leads to their paedophilic debauchment via a long, slow, and seemingly ritualized striptease. It is only later revealed that all three children are murdered, along with a cast of other victims whose corpses are removed from the boat, wrapped in plastic, and lined up along the riverside. Where this story turns to splatter, however, is in the seduction of a hitchhiking sailor and stylized "sexual proletarian," a man whose hat reads "Potemkin."

At the culmination of their romance the captain and the sailor have sex in a pit of refined white sugar. The scene is depicted with a roving camera that zooms, tilts, and pans across their writhing bodies. "Sugar is dangerous," she warns, twice. "Sugar is dangerous." She then enacts a brutal *coitus interruptus*, biting a chunk of flesh from each of his shoulders and stabbing him in the stomach with a long carving knife. The stabbing is shown in close-up: first his blood wells to the surface of the sugar, then she twists the knife, gouging a wound whose blood now coagulates into purplish mud. He chuckles to death and, grinning, she conceals his body in the sugar. The metaphor is simple enough, but what gives the scene its force is the horrific subtext, the way it codifies affectively that the sickly sweetness of post-socialist ideology conceals that which is just plain sick. As the captain-turned-murderess puts it: "Don't stay here. This boat is full of corpses."

Lastly, I want to include a brief parenthesis on one film that is occasionally cited as a precursor to some of those we will be looking at in subsequent chapters, and especially when it comes to torture porn. Pier Paolo Pasolini's *Salò, or the 120 Days of Sodom* from 1975 is one of the great anti-fascist propaganda films. Here we will skip ahead to its final minutes, which depict the mutilation of several children at the hands of their abductors. This violence is witnessed as point-of-view iris shots looking down from the second story of a villa into a courtyard where the tortures take place: a head is scalped, an eye gouged, a tongue pulled, and flesh is whipped, burnt, and branded. In short, bodies splatter.

And yet, the way this sequence is shot, as well as its relationship to the film's overall narrative, distinguishes it from the exemplary scenes of violence directed by Godard and Makavejev. Whereas those other directors both rely on rapid-fire montage and unsparing close-ups to mine the affective intensity of gore, here the torture is seen from a distance in medium and long shots. Emphasizing that distance, one of the fascist libertines watches the violence through opera glasses and, in one instance, he flips them around the wrong way so that in the binocular distortion the cinematic apparatus intrudes on the fantasy space of the sadistic spectacle. Pasolini's film – and this is the genius in its portrayal of violence – is constructed in such a way that we cannot enjoy it, that we cannot indulge in visual pleasure, and this is because the violence he depicts belongs exclusively to fascism.

While Eisenstein, as well as Godard and Makavejev after him, present violence using a populist aesthetic as a kind of propaganda for anti-capitalist insurgency, for Pasolini here it is the miserably logical conclusion of a very specific political sequence. There is nothing spectacular in this, nothing pleasing or affirmative. Bertolt Brecht would have called this an alienation effect. *Verfremdungseffekt*. So writes the film's most sensitive viewer and the worthiest inheritor of its legacy, Austrian director Michael Haneke, comparing it precisely to the kinds of film in which this book is more interested: "They may be scary, but they're still a turn-on. *Salò* won't turn you on at all – it will turn your stomach."[49]

This chapter draws to a close by suggesting that the common sense shared between these thinkers and these films is that splatter conveys something integral about the experience of humankind's conversion into labour power, about how we all inhabit the moving contradiction and that splatter might therefore put truth to the multiform mutilations attending this process. But, within this frame, splatter also speaks to a way forward, a way that is steeped in horror. This isn't just Lenin, with whom we began. It's also Marx, but not the Marx of *Capital*. This time it's Marx of the *Manifesto*:

> In depicting the most general phases of the development of the proletariat, we traced the more or less veiled civil war, raging within existing society, up to the point where that war breaks out into open revolution, and where the violent overthrow of the bourgeoisie lays the foundation for the sway of the proletariat.[50]

That is what we are seeing in splatter. Civil war unveiled.

Marx, Marxists, and Marxist filmmakers all know that capitalism is its own kind of horror film, and that an equally horrific confrontation will be this film's only suitable *dénouement*. Which leaves us with some big questions. To what extent does the generic form of splatter and its various motifs retain memory of these antecedents? Are there moments when an inherited and inborn critique becomes transparent, actively shaping a cinematic art that both knowingly and unknowingly responds to the dynamics of capitalism? Do popular splatter films offer a glimpse into that civil war "raging within existing society" and its revolutionary potential? These questions will inform our response to splatter from the contexts in which that genre has reached the high-tide marks of its popularity, when it threatens to burst upon the crumbling edifice of an American empire.

Second Intermission

Castration Porn

Back to the fabled video stores of my adolescence. It's now a few years later and I am in my mid-teens. Despite whatever rearrangements have taken place in shelving, horror is still right next to the porn, and both are sequestered off into a shady corner away from the more respectable genres. This spatial arrangement makes conceptual sense. Decades before the "torture porn" descriptor would achieve ubiquity, splatter had already become mindful of its kinship with the skin flicks, and some video covers exploited this proximity for all they could. Tits and ass accompanied chainsaws and hatchets.

One image stands out in memory as exemplary of this. A woman is shown from behind, facing away from us and into dense woodland. In her right hand a bloodied knife, clutched by the blade. It's hard to tell what she is wearing: a torn garment hangs off of her shoulders exposing the entirety of her back. Its high-cut bottom cleaves to the bodily curvature, covering little and vanishing into the crevice. The scrapes and bruises on her back fade into overexposed brightness. Signs of struggle. Visually, at least, this design banked more on smut than horror, in keeping as it is with the rough aesthetic of Russ Meyer-esque sexploitation. The model isn't even the starring actor, namely Camille Keaton (Buster's grand-niece), but someone with a shapelier figure. Rumour has it that a young Demi Moore posed for the promotional shot. "This woman," the accompanying text informs us in stuttering ellipses, "has just... cut, chopped, broken and burned four men beyond recognition... But no jury in America would ever convict her!" Beneath all of this, the title is announced in red, capitalized letters, slanting across the foot of the image: I SPIT ON YOUR GRAVE.

I recall picking up this video on multiple occasions, but never renting it until I had exhausted just about all of the films that more obviously marketed themselves as splatter. It just wasn't as interesting. If asked to speculate on why this was the case, I would say that it might have been because for me at this point in time sex had become more a part of everyday life and, be that as it may, the fantasies upheld by the rigid iconography of porn seemed both uninspired and unrealistic. This is not to impose any sort of moral or political judgment on porn. Rather, it is to recall that, for me back then, porn's reductive take on desire and eroticism seemed impossibly workmanlike and missionary. It was unrealistic precisely because it was so boring. Gore, by contrast, presented itself as radically anterior to everyday life but, nevertheless, it also seemed to contain some kernel of truth about the way things are. Realistic because imaginative.

The specificity of my puerile taste appears to have solidified in the nebulous interchange between realism and fantasy. Though I was neither aroused nor repulsed by filmic porn, at least not in any remarkable or memorable way, I can also say with even greater confidence that no part of me wanted to see its synthesis with horror. That would shift the resulting film from merely uninteresting to emphatically unappealing. And so, even if that cover, with its offer of Demi Moore's well-formed ass, was designed precisely to woo teenaged boys like me, the obvious market for a lot of horror, that is not what drew me in. Rather, I watched the film because my obsessive sense of completionism meant that I had to see all of the available horror films, this one included.

Like *Blood Sucking Freaks*, with which this film shared its Australian distributor and so too the format of its cover, *I Spit on Your Grave* went through several alternate titles before its definitive release in 1980. It first previewed in 1978 as *Day of the Woman*, and subsequently screened as both *I Hate Your Guts* and *The Rape and Revenge of Jennifer Hill*. As that literal title indicates, this is indeed a rape-revenge film. In it, Jennifer Hills is a fiction writer from Manhattan who rents an isolated property on the Housatonic River in Connecticut, in order to pen her first novel without the interruptions of city life. She immediately attracts the attention of four local men—Johnny, Stanley, Andy, and Matthew—who are either unemployed or working menial jobs at the gas station and grocery store. They kidnap Jennifer and humiliate, strip, rape, sodomize, and beat her. Whereas the gore films I enjoyed all seemed to play their carnage for a kind of stupid pleasure, embracing their own absurdity, in this case there was none of that: only ultra-realistic punishment meted out for a record-setting twenty-five minutes and without a soundtrack to detract from the hellish actuality of it all. Video-*vérité*. Then, after a prolonged physical recovery, Jennifer steels herself and systematically exterminates all four assailants: Matthew is garrotted, Johnny castrated, Andy axed and drowned, and Stanley mutilated with an outboard motor. All of which is, suffice to say, fittingly cathartic.

So much of this film's force is in its visual grammar, in the way it frames its narrative, and in what that framing does to the relationships between gender and violence. It is common knowledge that horror films, and especially splatter, tend to privilege a masculine if not male perspective. Not only does horror share its retail space with porn; the two retain a near interchangeable vantage on human bodies. Regrettably for someone as enthusiastic about splatter as I always have been, it is largely because of this generic articulation that in gore films women are disproportionately made the objects of violence.

From the outset, and this is just as true of the cover image as it is of the film's opening scenes, we are told that this kind of visual chauvinism is what to expect from the present offering. Pre-empting the clichéd point-of-view shots in which Michael Myers or Jason Voorhees spy their quarry from the concealed middle-distance, we are given a voyeuristic sequence (shot mostly from Matthew's perspective) in which Jennifer strips off and swims naked in the river. And yet, the masculine perspective lasts for no longer than this first of three acts. Hereafter, the perspective belongs to Jennifer. Precisely this, its feminized viewpoint, is what makes the film so radically unique. During the second act, for Jennifer's torture, we are given third-person views of her body and of the crimes inflicted upon it, but very few approximations of the rapists' vantage. Instead, the prevailing view is hers. We are repeatedly forced to watch screens filled with the looming faces of her rapists grunting and snarling. In fact, during the rape scenes the only embodied, point-of-view shots are taken from the victim. That these scenes are so deeply unpleasant to watch seems to be rewarded in the final act, during which Jennifer exacts her revenge.

Though the means by which Jennifer dispatches the rapists adheres to the archetype of any given slasher film, with our sympathies tied firmly to the victim-hero, at least one scene would find a happy home in splatter – and, interestingly enough, it is this scene which seems most reflexive about the articulation of violence, gender, and the economy, as well as about the formal relationship between gore and porn.

Jennifer stands completely naked before a mirror, pinning up her hair. This prolonged attention to cosmetic appearance emphasizes the exposure of her body. The shot is taken from just over her left shoulder, so that the skin of her back takes up the most screen space, and serves as a spatial double for the mirror: she is on the right side of the shot, her reflection on the left, and between the two images, front and back, is the diminutive form of her erstwhile assailant, Johnny, seated in a bathtub and covered from the waist down with bubbles. She seems to be watching herself watching him. She asks about his family and about his friends, her rapists. "They're not my friends," he tells her. "You know they hang on me like leeches. Goofing off all the time. I really despise people that don't work. Get into trouble too easily." A strange reminder, this: that he works, and that she might not, and that he supports a wife and two children, whereas she does not. Strange because it seems calculated to generate sympathy for a man deserving of so little, and who will be shown even less. Jennifer turns toward the bath. The right side of the shot is now empty, filled only with off-white wallpaper, as she steps down into the bathtub. She splashes water over Johnny and the scene cuts to a medium shot, side on, of the two. She confesses to murdering one of the rapists, Mathew, and explains precisely how she did so. He laughs it off as her hands roam lower and lower, below the water, pleasuring him by hand and out of view from the camera's eye.

It all seems tastefully erotic, like something out of a softcore film. We then see her right hand reaching down besides the bathtub and lifting a long carving knife, which had been concealed beneath a towel. Back to the medium shot. The knife goes down into the water. "Oh, fuck yeah, that's fantastic." Her arms motion faster, she leans in, and the knife emerges from the bubbles trailing a thin streak of blood. "That's so sweet it's painful." A torrent of deep red jets from his crotch. The money shot: softcore becomes hardcore. He bleeds everywhere, holding onto the severed stump, spraying the bathroom crimson, smearing it across tiles and porcelain.

High-pitched screaming. She sets the knife down in a sink and calmly leaves the bathroom, locking the door behind her. We follow her downstairs, where she drops the pin on a record whose operatic strains compete with and soon overwhelm the shouting and screaming and crashing that emanates from upstairs and off-screen. The shot slowly, perhaps even gently, zooms in on Jennifer's face.

Some feminist film theory will help make sense of what we are seeing here. Carol Clover's 1987 essay "Her Body, Himself" remains the single most influential piece of academic writing on horror cinema, and for good reason.[51] In its argument, which focuses exclusively on the slasher film, Clover specifies that this genre

> not despite but exactly because of its crudity and compulsive repetitiveness gives us a clearer picture of current sexual attitudes, at least among the segment of the population that forms its erstwhile audience, than do the legitimate products of the better studios.[52]

In explaining why a genre whose primary audience is composed of young men so frequently promotes female "victim-heroes," Clover posits a kind of oedipal surrogacy, but it is a surrogacy which the films' themselves seem to obviate.

> Abject terror may still be gendered feminine, but the willingness of one immensely popular current genre to represent the hero as an anatomical female would seem to suggest that at least one of the traditional marks of heroism, triumphant self-rescue, is no longer simply gendered masculine.[53]

The reason why this claim is so tentative, why that willingness would only "seem to suggest" recalibration, is because the means by which the female victim becomes the female hero is by assuming the male gaze as her own and acquiring a symbolic phallus, such as we saw in the bathroom scene above. While this is a bracingly clear-eyed description of the slasher film, of which the present rape-revenge movie is exemplary, the gender politics of splatter are even less progressive. Whereas slasher films are at least suggestive of a progressive take on gender relations, the overwhelming majority of splatter films veer into outright and indefensible misogyny.

One of the reasons for this misogyny is splatter's proximity to porn. If there are similarities between porn and horror in general, or between pornography and slasher films, in splatter that similarity results from historical contiguity. As we are going to see in the subsequent chapter, splatter's popular formation emerged as an offshoot from porn, and it definitely retains the traces of that origin. Without getting into the manifold polemics surrounding feminist discussions of porn, it should be obvious enough that, at least since the advent of hardcore, mainstream porn has favoured a masculine perspective. It fetishizes and, in that fetishism, it objectifies. That is to say, visual pleasure in porn is the result of a male gaze recasting feminine bodies as, at best, passive objects for penetration or, at worst, receptacles for degradation. Though it has been debated at length whether or not this kind of objectification is a formal expression of misogyny, the point here is that, when you transpose a masculine perspective on the female body out of a genre whose visual pleasure is tied to sex into a genre whose visual pleasure is tied to violence, the result is going to be male violence against women. While this is no ironclad law, and it is certainly not true of all splatter, it nevertheless appears to be functioning determinately within the majority of gore films. I never realized this as a teenager, but the feeling was always there.

I Spit on Your Grave is a corrective to all of that, and we should appreciate its brutality on those terms. However, in subverting generically programmed misogyny, this film resorts to a reactionary view of its own, pertaining to class. Its narrative is, to quote from Clover, "an almost crystalline example of the double-axis revenge plot so popular in modern horror: the revenge of the woman on her rapist, and the revenge of the city on the country."[54] That division, between the city and the country, is just as much a division between rich and poor. Between an urbane middle class and the primitive lumpen. And, in this case, we find ourselves cheering for the resolutely bourgeois victim-hero against a band of small-town thugs turned rapists. Here is Clover's account of the film's two axes:

> That is, with a member of the gender underclass (a woman) representing the economic overclass (the urban rich) and members of the gender overclass (males) representing the economic underclass (the rural poor), a feminist politics of rape has been deployed in the service of class and racial guilt. Raped and battered, the haves can rise to annihilate the have-nots – all in the name of feminism.[55]

There is, in this sense, a political opposition between two sub-generic forms of horror cinema: if the slasher film, with its conservative class politics, settles the score in terms of gender representation, perhaps we can say the same thing about splatter and class, that gore films encourage the recalibration of values in opposition to capitalism and against the legions of its beneficiaries. Unavoidable, however, is the contradictory consciousness encoded in the formal tension between porn and gore. In splatter, members of an economic underclass (disenfranchised workers) representing the gender overclass (male) target members of the economic overclass (the urban rich) primarily represented as the gender underclass (women). For all its economic intelligence, splatter has some insoluble limitations. Foremost of these: its regressive treatment of women.

Chapter 3

American Fleshfeast

An Egyptian Cannibal in Florida

A woman with big hair enters a blue-lit room. Kettledrums beat slowly, modulating between two inharmonious notes. She walks to the bathroom and looks at herself in the mirror. The shot closes in on a transistor radio. "And now some tragic local news. We have a report of another tragic murder tonight. A young girl has been found dead in Roger's Park." Cut to an over-the-shoulder shot of the woman's mirrored reflection, hands to face and clearly alarmed. "The body was badly mutilated. Because of these murders police request that all women stay inside their homes after dark..." The radio repeats this instruction and the woman turns it off. She strips down and sets a leather-bound book aside the bathtub. The kettledrums hasten slightly and the shot lingers over the book's title: *Ancient Weird Religious Rights*. The woman is now in the bathtub, concealed from the neck down with bubbles. A shadow fills the frame. The shadow's source is revealed with a series of jump-cuts bridged together by the woman's distorted scream: a suited man, with a shock of greying hair and a set of inscrutably bushy eyebrows, knife raised. Norman Bates, minus the dowdy frock and acting chops. The shots blur toward imperceptibility, the scream ends, the kettledrums are replaced by a synthesized organ, and the man brings the blade up toward his own face, grinning insanely at the chunks of flesh it has skewered. We are shown the woman's body, bleeding profusely from an eviscerated eye-socket. The camera pans from right to left, holding to the man's perspective, from that ocular wound down her torso, which is now partially exposed from the bubbles, and toward her legs. Cut to the man's eyes in extreme close-up. His gaze broadcasts lunacy. Then comes the real gore: several shots of rough butchery, culminating in the removal of the woman's left leg from just above the knee, followed by a shot of her bloodied hand sliding down the tiles and then, finally, a close-up on the stump, which is semi-submerged in bathwater and exhibiting its blood, bone, and sinew. Fade to an image of the Sphinx and the Great Pyramid in Giza, set before an unnaturally blue backdrop and over which the film's title is projected in dripping red sludge: BLOOD FEAST.

The consensus among film historians is that with this scene, opening a film released in 1963, splatter first learned to recognize itself. Some have suggested that Jennifer's bathtub castration of Johnny is an homage to Alfred Hitchcock, to the infamous shower scene, but it's really a riposte to what we just have witnessed here. Directed by Herschell Gordon Lewis, produced by David F. Friedman, and written through collaboration between the two, this low-budget, independent film was the inaugural moment when mutilation finally became the message. Splatter's *urtext*. Lewis would be first to approve of this characterization, often referring to *Blood Feast* as his "Walt Whitman poem," claiming that "it's no good, but it's the first of its type and therefore deserves a certain position."[56] Its plot follows a specialist caterer, Fuad Ramses, who murders young women so as to include their severed limbs in exotic cuisine and whose labour of killing is undertaken as sacrificial offering to the Egyptian Goddess, Ishtar. That image of the pyramid is, however, not the original, in Egypt, but a model replica from outside a hotel in Miami, Florida, the film's garishly vibrant setting.

With visibly low-end production and a threadbare narrative, this film dedicates almost all of its technical and stylistic energy to the depiction of graphic dismemberment, of which a brief catalogue will suffice: cerebral matter and bloody coagulum explode from the top of a skull; a tongue is severed, bringing several inches of muscle out with it; a heart is carved from its chest and crushed in hand – and all of this is, utilizing those formal conventions established by Eisenstein, captured as montage and framed in close-up. With this kind of imagery, presented in the oversaturated colours and with the vertiginous cutting of that opening scene, this film would set the gold standard for American splatter. Beginning here, in Miami and with Lewis, this chapter sets some of the most popular of the early splatter films against their historical backdrop, looking at some of the ways they tap into the economic crisis unfurling around them, and how they use that crisis to fan the flames of anti-capitalist aggression.

First, however, a note on visual grammar and generic ancestry, which will help us specify what *I Spit on Your Grave*, released about a decade later in 1978, would react against. Near the conclusion of *Blood Feast*, a camera tracks horizontally to take in every inch of a woman's stripped and flayed body, from head to toe, after she has been whipped to death. It repeats the panning movement from the opening scene, but this time the shot's perspective belongs to two male detectives investigating the murders. In the camera's slowly revelatory movements, and in its resolutely masculine perspective on the female body, both of these shots are emblematic of what Laura Mulvey once described as "scopophilia," or the pleasure taken in gazing upon another person as an erotic object. "The presence of woman is an indispensable element of spectacle in normal narrative film," contends Mulvey, "yet her visual presence tends to work against the development of a story line, to freeze the flow of action in moments of erotic contemplation."[57] With shots like these as combined with the pronounced affection for close-ups on bodily wounds, it is not without significance that Lewis and his co-conspirator Friedman, as well as several of the other pioneers of splatter, learned their trade by directing sexploitation flicks.

There are historical reasons for the continuity between porn and this kind of horror, in that splatter became self-aware and popular only when, in the 1960s, Hollywood absorbed softcore pornography into its own more glamorous productions. The old smut directors responded by providing scenes of gore the likes of which mainstream cinema had never seen, shot with an affection for bodily detail which at that time was more familiar to porn than horror. It should therefore be no mystery as to why there are some obvious formal consistencies between splatter and porn, both of which specialize in the production of fantasy images designed to be visually and above all viscerally affective. As Steven Shaviro puts it, using language similar to Eisenstein: "They both are about things happening to human bodies, bodies on an intense sensorial level,"[58] and this sensorial intensity is achieved not only by the depicted content but also by the technical decisions made in the framing and editing of that content. What makes the relationship between splatter and porn important here is that both utilize remarkably similar techniques to produce a visually fragmented body in which limbs and entrails and openings (which can be either orifices or wounds, depending on your genre, or both, in extreme instances of either) are lensed separately and in close-up before their sequencing into montage. Like porn, the splatter film articulates an aesthetic of disaggregated bodies, and the work of both genres is to reify those bodies and their specific organs into affectively charged fetish-objects.

We are now at one of those moments when a feminist critique of the horror film dovetails with economic materialism, a point from which we can begin thinking clearly about how the genre's over-theorized visual pleasure relates to its political economy, and that it does so at the cost of a liberating or even acceptable politics of gender. To do this, we first need to think about the characters themselves, about what they embody, and about how the film frames them. In a comprehensive chapter on Lewis' film, Kjetil Rødje suggests that its carefully curated selection of victims, all of whom are beautiful bourgeois women, is fuelled not only by masculine sexual fantasy but also by a declaration of class hostility (which melds reprehensibly enough with that masculine fantasy):

> When considering the composition of the original audience for these movies, it seems plausible that the films' victims do not share the same demographic profile as the typical audience members. Hence, audiences are not invited to identify and sympathize with the victims slaughtered on-screen. Rather, the films feed into already existing biases, connecting with possible feelings of resentment directed towards more privileged social groups. The victims' vanity and stupidity further stir this resentment. The portrayals confirm stereotypes and reinforce perceptions

about social groups economically and culturally distant from the audience members.[59]

Unlike these vain and vapid caricatures of social privilege, in films directed by Lewis the aggressors tend to be culturally marginalized and economically disenfranchised. Their ranks include intransigently confederate hillbillies, down-and-out artists, and abused strippers. Ramses fits the bill of an immigrant worker, undertaking thankless labour at a small grocery store while continuing to worship the old gods of his homeland, Egypt. Moreover, the very idea of immigrant labour landing hard upon class divisions takes on added meaning in relation to the film's setting of Miami, Florida in the 1960s, where social structures were reshuffling in the wake of the Cuban Revolution of 1959.

Specifically, Fidel Castro's seizure of power from Fulgencio Batista in the name of socialism generated a transnational exchange of immigrants and of immigrant labour, in which most of the Miami-based Cubans returned home, while many of the middle and upper-class Cubans moved to Florida. The result, in Miami, was an enormous culturally and linguistically foreign working-class population – numbering over four hundred thousand – from whose members the American government would recruit for its war against the socialist state, which came to a blood-spattered climax in the Bay of Pigs Invasion of 1961. It is thus that Miami was unique as the American city in which an ethnically divided working class came to exist under the sign of a geographically proximate socialist revolution.

By preying exclusively on bourgeois women, and by subjecting them to the violent depredations faced by a modern working class as well as by an ancient slave class, Ramses putatively enacts something like a socialist reversal on this film's highly stratified relations of production. This reversal is made narratively possible by way of a formal contract, made between his employer, Dorothy Freemont, and her worker, the killer Ramses. After the opening murder, the next time we see Ramses he is working behind the counter in his small, underpopulated grocery store. He is approached by an ostentatiously dressed, heavily made-up, and emphatically waspy woman, Freemont, who is making arrangements to host that singularly bourgeois of all social events: a dinner party. "I want something unusual," she claims, "something totally different." When Ramses suggests an authentic Egyptian feast, she responds gaily: "Why, that would be fine! That would be perfect! My daughter Suzette is a student of Egyptian culture, Mr Ramses. She'd just love it!" With mother and daughter Freemont bearing all the insignia of bourgeois privilege, and in stark contrast to the working foreigner, splatter thus introduces itself to the mainstream American audience as a politically charged satire against the leisure class.

If the truth of satire is that it always comes at the expense of another, that it is always militantly oppositional, in this film gore itself acquires precisely that kind of satirical force, encouraging us to choose sides. For it is here that violence is dished out along the familiar lines of class warfare, with the alienated worker gleefully dismembering the embodiments of economic privilege, his employers. Recall from previous chapters that the value of each commodity is indexical to the labour exploited in its production, and that value is therefore made up of the primal substance, *Gallerte*, the coagulated bodies and brains and spirit of innumerable workers. In this film, the eponymous feast is a commodity whose narrative task is to anchor the relations of production under capitalism, and to submit those relations to a triumphantly socialist reversal. Here the daughters of a ruling class are forcefully subjected to the full-blooded reprisal of the male worker whose labour has been hired on their behalf, for their dinner party, with their severed body parts baked into that titular commodity: the authentic blood feast.

Though we are never encouraged to identify with Ramses, who is equally if not more ridiculous than all of his victims, the porn-indebted aesthetic nevertheless invites us to take great pleasure in his actions, to relish the murders and the butchery. The visual pleasure of gore films like and including this one is in their carnage – to adopt the vocabulary of hardcore porn, the money shots here are those of maiming and mutilation – and, though we do not identify with the aggressor as a character, we are certainly paying to see the outcome of his aggression, those violent scenes which attract every ounce of the film's technical competence and aesthetic exuberance.

Unlike the film's expositive sequences – which are clunky as all hell, shot through with dialogic senility, and invariably depicted in formally conservative static medium shots – the murders frequently utilize a very specific and highly stylized visual choreography. The scenes of gore intercut between close-ups and medium shots edited together into montage sequences through which the victim is transformed and transvalued into the genre-imagery of their severed limbs and eviscerated innards. "The focus," notes Rødje, "is on the before-and-after: we see the killer as he attacks, his hands as he fondles the body parts, and then the mauled body of the victim."[60] And so, even without identification, in that focus we come to share the political perspective of what he represents. We are invited to share in his pleasure. We too are asked to enjoy the murders. Perhaps that is why so much of this film's opening sequence is focused on Ramses' eyes.

The film's ending makes this political allegiance reasonably clear. At the Freemont residence – a lush apartment – Ramses requests the cooperation of that young lady in whose name the feast is given, Suzette, so as to ensure real authenticity. He directs her onto the kitchen bench where, with eyes shut, she is instructed to raise her white-gloved arms heavenward and to repeat several incantations. The scene is excruciatingly protracted in its teasing of imminent bloodshed. Suzette keeps sitting up, forgetting her lines, giggling, never aware of the damocletian fate hanging immediately above her. Finally, Ramses raises a machete and, in the pause before he strikes, Suzette's mother, Dorothy, interrupts. Everybody screams. Ramses flees the building. Two police officers arrive. "Mrs. Freemont, I'm afraid this feast is evidence of murder." "Oh dear," she reacts. "The guests will have to eat hamburgers for dinner tonight."

Whatever disappointment attends this scene and its refusal to deliver one final spectacle of gore is redoubled in Ramses' own death, which offers little in the way of visual pleasure. With the police in pursuit, Ramses limps his way into a sanitation plant where he hurls himself suicidally into the back of a dump truck, which crushes his body completely off-screen and leaves only a bloody smear. The ideological charge resides in the presentational imbalance between two kinds of violence. Two kinds of anti-climax: one is suspenseful and dramatic; the other is simply dull. The film encourages us to enjoy and even desire one kind of murder, when Ramses lovingly takes out members of the leisure class, but it has much less to do with another. We might relish the slayings of the bourgeoisie, but the death of their assailant is set up to be much less affecting. Perhaps this is not surprising, given Lewis is more than just adopting the visual grammar of porn: whether consciously or not, he is also directing his films using the technical conventions established almost half a century earlier by Eisenstein. Here, at the point of splatter's emergence in American cinema, it has clearly retained the memory not only of its pornographic origins but also of its revolutionary prehistory.

Out of the Emporium and into the Abattoir

All of that establishes right from the inaugural moment an anti-capitalist subtext for the American splatter film. But if, in this case, the anti-capitalism remains relatively inconspicuous, if it is still deeply subtextual, one of the reasons for that is the historical climate. The early 1960s were, on the face of it, a boom time for capitalism, especially in the United States, where the basic structures of accumulation held their integrity. This was a period defined by economic expansion as enabled by the internationalisation of industrial production, and not yet antagonized internally by the moving contradiction, but only externally by the proliferation of anti-capitalist states, newly in Cuba and Vietnam but persistently in the Soviet Union. We were still basking in what Robert Brenner once called the "Long Boom," which would last from the end of World War II up until the collapse of the Bretton Woods system in 1971, the oil crisis of 1973, and the 1973-74 stock market crash, all of which led to recession.[61]

However, the expansionism of the 1950s and 60s only set

the scene for the crisis to follow:

> its very unfolding resulted in a major intensification of competitive pressures on each and every governmental and business organization of the capitalist world-economy and in a consequent massive withdrawal of money capital from trade and production.[62]

In the early 1970s, economic expansion was met by stagflation, when accumulation was driven downward by the decline of industrial manufacture's rate of profit. The moving contradiction thus revealed itself. And though – as we will see in the following chapters – this signal crisis was displaced by a shift from manufacture into finance, from a productive to a speculative economy, that very shift nevertheless led to the further extirpation of industrial labour, primarily through foreclosures, offshoring, and mass redundancy.

While *Blood Feast* took place in the build-up to this crisis, the second film we will look at occupies the crisis itself and deploys splatter as a response to the resultant restructurings of capital. Tobe Hooper's early masterpiece, *The Texas Chain Saw Massacre*, was released amidst the recession in 1974 and it knowingly inhabits this context. This film is about a group of five young people travelling across Texas to investigate the necrophilic vandalism of a cemetery containing familial graves. Due to a nationwide gas shortage (the same one mentioned in *Blood Sucking Freaks*) they find themselves stranded, confined to their ancestral homestead, a ramshackle building in Travis County just outside of Austin, and that night all but one is murdered by a neighbouring family of cannibals. The cannibal family comprises three brothers – known to us only as Cook, the Hitchhiker, and Leatherface – and their barely-animate, zombified grandfather. They are, in Robin Wood's account, "representatives of an exploited and degraded proletariat," brutalized by circumstance and now biting back with a vengeance.[63]

From within this narrative, the film presents its horrors as indexical to the circumstances faced by the industrial labour force in the early 1970s. Here a slaughterhouse foreclosure and a petrol shortage combine to generate the conditions of possibility for scenes of gore, which are variously punctuated by tableaux redolent of the ongoing war against a socialist state in Vietnam. This redolence is only strengthened by the film's more recent remake, which backfills the narrative with a plot about enlisting to go fight the Viet Cong. Hooper has always insisted that his film is a direct response to the social unrest of its historical context. "We were out of gas in the country at the time," he has recently said, "and it boiled up out of those times. It's all true, the content of the film, actually. People were put out of jobs, they were out of gas at the gas station."[64] With this film, so much more so than *Blood Feast*, gore emanates up and outward from the mode of production.

The Texas Chain Saw Massacre is, at its heart, the story of unemployed abattoir workers applying the skills of their trade to the butchery of humans. An early scene makes this connection explicitly. The van in which our five victims travel passes what one, the wheelchair bound Franklin, points out is the old slaughterhouse, "where grandpa used to sell his cattle," which leads to a conversation about the technological acceleration of industrial butchery. "See those buildings there," we are told. "That's where they kill 'em. They bash 'em in the head with a big sledge hammer." Cut to a non-diegetic medium shot of a cow, foaming at the mouth, and then to several still and travelling shots through the slaughterhouse, culminating in a lengthy panning shot that follows the van from right to left across the frame with the cattle in the foreground, thereby forging an association between the van's occupants and the soon-to-be-slaughtered livestock. The bovine montage is reminiscent of Eisenstein.

Back to the van, we are given a narrative rendition of how the cattle are slaughtered. "They'd start squealin' and freakin' out and they'd have to come up and bash 'em two or three times, and then sometimes it wouldn't kill 'em. They'd skin 'em sometimes before they were even dead." We are told that this process has been outmoded by a "big air-gun that shoots a bolt into their skull and then retracts," which is accompanied by a kind of air-guitar re-enactment, with Franklin repeatedly punching through an open palm, as though to emphasize the speed of its operation. What we are hearing described here is the means by which the embodiments of productive labour were made superfluous to industry during the 1970s, replaced by technology in such a way as to temporarily increase profits by cutting expenditure but, simultaneously, diminishing the value of production by decreasing the role of labour therein. In other words, this conversation perfectly illustrates the moving contradiction.

The effect of the moving contradiction on the carriers of labour power, the now unemployed workers, is enunciated in the same scene when they collect a bloodstained hitchhiker, who gives off all the vibes of a deeply traumatized and psychically scattered war veteran. "My brother worked there," strictly in the past tense. "My grandfather too. My family's always been in meat." He defends the sledgehammer against the airgun as a matter of employment. "The new way," he says, "people put out of jobs." Then things get weird. He produces a handful of crumpled polaroids snapped within the slaughterhouse. Dead cattle with shattered skulls. Emblems of a morbid nostalgia. "I was the killer!" he announces, merrily, before providing a recipe for what he calls "headcheese," but which we have heard Marx describe as *Gallerte*. The recipe:

> They take the head and they boil it, except for the tongue, and scrape all the flesh away from the bone. They use everything, they throw nothing away. They use jaws, muscles, and the eyes, and the ligaments... They boil the nose and the gums down to a big jelly of fat. It's really good. Do you like it?

Things go from weird to worse very quickly. The hitchhiker slices open his own palm with a straight-razor, takes a photograph of Franklin, lights up the photograph using gunpowder, slashes Franklin's hand, and – when thrown out – smears a mixture of his and Franklin's blood on the side of the van. Amongst other things, and beyond the shock of that first encounter between the lumpen underclass and the bourgeois sons and daughters of land- and cattle-owners, this early scene invites us to think about how capitalism's moving contradiction shapes lived experience, casting slaughterhouse workers out of their workplace and onto the highways. It also serves as a portent for what will happen when the carriers of living labour power are forced to pursue their work beyond the sphere of industrial production, a place where they are no longer needed. In this crisis everyone boils down to a big jelly of fat. Another blood feast is in the offing.

The film's first scenes of violence make good on all of that by allowing one of the jobless slaughterhouse workers to murder two of the travellers, Kirk and Pam, in precisely the way described above, as though they are cattle for the slaughter. After venturing into a nearby house, Kirk is drawn by animal squeals down a dimly lit hallway to stand before an open door, which looks through to a red wall decorated by cow skulls. He trips and looks up in time for us to see, from his perspective and for just a split second, a hulking man in a black tie and butcher's apron, wearing a mask made of skin, raising a mallet up above his head. Meet Leatherface, to whom we sold that chainsaw back in Chapter 1. The camera cuts to the end of the hallway, watching from a distance, as the mallet comes down and cracks Kirk's skull. Kirk falls to the floor, seizures violently, and is struck again. This is shown in a series of close-ups accompanied by more squeals, not from an animal but from the butcher. Kirk is dragged beyond the threshold and the door, which has the metal thickness of an industrial meat locker, is slammed shut.

The following shot follows Kirk's hotpants-accoutred girlfriend, Pam, from an ass-emphatic low-angle as she too disappears into the house. This truly virtuosic shot, which will be remade decades later by Eli Roth, recalls splatter's pornographic origins and stresses its gendered viewpoint. She turns left from the hallway instead of opening the steel door and finds herself in a room filled with calcified bones, both animal and human, arranged into ghoulish decorations, made into furniture, and strung up from the ceiling. As she tries to flee, the steel door is flung open. Leatherface catches her, picks her up by the waist, and carries her back to the room into which Kirk disappeared. We see this room from the cornice diagonal to the doorway, framing it crookedly and from behind one of two meat hooks overlooking a large refrigerator. We then see, from the perspective of the doorway, Pam carried to the hooks, hoisted up, and hung to bleed out. Meat hook through the spine. Kirk is in the foreground sprawled out on a table. Leatherface paces the room before collecting the eponymous chainsaw from a nearby bench. It starts up to a deafening buzz. The camera zooms inquisitively, at different times on both Leatherface and Pam. Kirk is butchered off-screen.

The most celebrated academic explanation of this film belongs once again to Carol Clover, and it focuses on the role of Sally, Franklin's sister, as the massacre's sole survivor and the film's "final girl." But I want to highlight a different aspect of Clover's account. For her, the preferred weaponry in horror films "would seem to suggest that closeness and tactility are also at issue," and so she reads these armaments psychosexually as "personal extensions of the body that bring the attacker and attacked into primitive, animalistic embrace."[65] My suggestion, a supplement to Clover's argument, is that splatter's reappropriation of power tools is also about class, and that its primitivism is born of a life spent in an increasingly superannuated manufacture-based economy.

If tools are used for artisanal manufacture, a kind of production that really would engineer an embrace between the worker and the object of labour, the tool can be thought of as an index to the evolution of capitalism out of artisanal manufacture and toward large-scale industry. When the bolt-gun and the mechanized killing box replace the sledgehammer and the chainsaw, the human labourer loses his place within the slaughterhouse. The tool, as opposed to the machine, exemplifies a nostalgic attachment to moments of pre-industrial manufacture, a nostalgia that registers most saliently in times of crisis when productive labour finds itself under erasure. Here and elsewhere the psychosexualized murder scenes all take place when the tools of labour are removed from a collapsing sphere of production and reinserted into new social relations.

Perhaps this, too, is why an attachment to the power tool reappears over and over again all throughout American splatter films in the 1970s and 80s, during the signal crisis. A playful sampling will help make the point: recall the chainsaw-hand with which Ash Williams fights off the Deadites in the Evil Dead trilogy; recall the chainsaw with which Estelle and John Collingwood avenge their daughter in *Last House on the Left* from 1972; recall Abel Ferrara's amped-up film of 1979, *Driller Killer*; and recall, too, the justificatory tagline of *Nail Gun Massacre* from 1985, which reveals a properly economic subtext to all of the above: "It's Cheaper than a Chainsaw!" It is thus that the moving contradiction, with its deracination of the industrial workforce, can be said to inform splatter in its choice of weaponry. Its fixed capital. Just how phallic that weaponry invariably is speaks exemplarily to the masculine viewpoint favoured by splatter's contradictory consciousness, and this time in a way that also suggests a male-dominated industry.

Like *Blood Feast*, cannibalism in *The Texas Chain Saw Massacre* is not only about eating the bourgeoisie, but also about forcing them to feast upon their own flesh and the flesh of their kin. The operative scene in which this dynamic plays out is the most aesthetically inventive in the film, when the final victim, Sally, is forced to the dinner table, where she joins all three brothers and their grandfather. With their guest bloody, bruised, and gagged, this is southern hospitality gone catastrophically awry. Sally's hand is sliced in extreme close-up and the ancient grandfather sucks the blood from her finger. We can presume that she faints, as we witness an extreme zoom-out, leaving the house in its entirety, followed by a slow focusing in on the full moon, after which Sally is shown in close-up regaining consciousness. The following shot is from her perspective, as it tilts up the table from a taxidermy chicken, to a human skull, to the desiccated grandfather. Cuts between Sally, screaming, and the family, mimicking her and howling with laughter. The montage picks up speed and the radically discontinuous and increasingly agitated jump-cuts emphasize the sheer horror of it all. Accompanying this, and while Sally screams and screams, the brothers argue about compelled work and the division of labour.

Hitchhiker:	He's nothin'. He's just a cook.
Cook:	Shut up you bitch hog!
Hitchhiker:	Me and Leatherface have to do all the work. He don't like it, ain't that right? You're just a cook!
Cook:	Shut your mouth! You don't understand.
Hitchhiker:	I understand you ain't nothing. Me and him do all the work!

Cook: Well I just can't take no pleasure in killing. There's just some things you gotta do. Don't mean you have to like it.

Sally cries. She pleads with her captors. The cutting accelerates again, over soundtrack blasts of discordant strings played too high. Everything about this scene is calculated for maximum horror. It denies any stable point of focus. It's as though the camera is undertaking the work of mutilation, violently dividing the body into its part-objects. Zoom to Sally's face. Cut to Cook. Back to Sally, this time closer. Back to Cook. Now Sally, zooming out. Hitchhiker. Sally. Zoom back in. Cut to her left eye. Bloodshot. A single tear. Hitchhiker, pulling faces. Sally's eyeball, in extreme close-up. Cook. Eyeball. Zoom to the iris. And closer still: so close you can count the veins.

"No sense in waiting." That was Cook, conflicted, wanting to end the torture. More jump-cuts, all on Sally and now cued to grating industrial noise. Metal on metal. Sally is forced to the ground, with her head in a bucket, so grandpa can try cracking her skull with the same mallet used on Kirk. This is an exercise in superannuated labour. "Grandpa's the best killer ever there was," we are told. "It never took more'n one lick they say. Did sixty in five minutes, once." What we are seeing here is the labour of disenfranchised abattoir workers made unemployable by the modernization of their industry and by the crisis in value caused by that very modernization. But for a few minutes their dining room is transformed into the slaughterhouse. Moreover, we are seeing the induction of the bourgeois subject into their way of being, an invitation to dinner on the other side of the class divide, out in the rural periphery where modernization is so obviously legible on its human subjects. In that earlier scene, the one in which abattoir labour is described from the van, Sally interrupts her brother's account of animal slaughter: "I like meat. Please change the subject." At this climactic moment, Sally has been sat down before a plate of sausages potentially made from Kirk and Pam, and with this she has finally been given an insight into the industrial production of meat.

Zombie Economics: The (Un)Death of Labour

If Lewis inaugurated the American splatter film and if, in the heat of an economic crisis, Hooper forged it into an outright critique of capitalism, it was George A. Romero who sustained that critique into the subsequent decades, while giving splatter its name. The term "splatter" was first used by Romero to describe the second film in his zombie cycle, *Dawn of the Dead*, released in 1978 and set during the ascendency of the undead's global domination. What makes Romero films splatter is their palpable love of violence, the manifestations of which take shape between the cannibalization of living humans and the extirpation of cannibalistic zombies.

Dawn of the Dead lives up to the descriptor within minutes of its opening, in a scene that is keyed into racial and class division and totally drenched in gore. The scene that introduces the film's two heroes, Roger and Peter, is focused on the clearing of a brownstone housing project, whose Puerto Rican and African American inhabitants defy martial law in refusing to surrender their dead. Any potential identification between the audience and the SWAT team's crypto-fascist operations is quickly thwarted when one openly bigoted officer lumbers into a kind of berserker frenzy, kicking in doors and murdering the civilian inhabitants. Famously, one of the shots depicts the explosion of a man's head when fired on by a shotgun. The shot only lasts a second or two but this, the exploding head, would become the signature effect of Tom Savini, who designed and implemented the gore for this film and for numerous others. Here we cannot tell if the man was human or zombie but, either way, the film's first splattering takes place at the hands of a white, authoritarian human and is inflicted on an immigrant man of unknown vitality. "The zombie for me is always the blue-collar monster," claims Romero. "He was always us."[66] While this scene begins to develop an association between the poor and the zombies, it also makes clear that the threat of splattering is omnipresent. In subsequent shots, zombies tear through the flesh of several survivors before being blasted to pieces. Here, in Romero's universe, everybody splatters.

It has become a well-worn truism, indeed a venerable cliché, that for Romero the zombie serves as an allegorical figure: "the zombie," writes Barry Keith Grant, "becomes a crucial metaphor of social relations for Romero as the prostitute for Godard."[67] Whilst true, that is not where this argument will end. Having said that, all of the films in Romero's zombie cycle exploit a specific fear or contradiction: of internecine race war, of consumerist stupefaction, of geopolitical antagonism, of proletariat uprisings, of media saturation, and so on. Complementary to this and present in the allegorical mix is the relatively familiar idea of zombie capitalism, a theory that suggests capitalism is itself an undead entity stalking the historical landscape with blind rapacity: "seemingly dead when it comes to achieving human goals and responding to human feelings, but capable of sudden spurts of activity that cause chaos all around."[68] In equal measure, it scarcely requires mentioning that the derisive name for Ronald Reagan's version of trickle-down economics, implemented in the early 1980s, shares its Haitian paradigm with the zombie–what we are dealing with in the wake of a signal crisis and in the emergence of neoliberalism is, of course, "voodoo economics."

And yet, while Romero's zombies are often allegorical vehicles for whatever antagonism, I want us to think more specifically about their consistently gruesome physiognomy and their appetite for human flesh, and how all of that might have more to teach us about economic history than the way their narratives variously encode the zombie as an avatar of race, consumerism, or geopolitics. What made Romero's zombies unique from their predecessors is that these are properly decomposing yet insatiably flesh-hungry cadavers equipped with sharp teeth and powerful jaws. In this way, because of their grotesque bodies, these zombies voraciously gnaw their way through the logic of figuration; their abject decay tends to expose the arbitrariness of any one figure, thereby thwarting reductive symbology.[69] What I want to accentuate here is the zombies' universalization of splatter, the way that in these films the bodies of both zombies and their victims are prone to disintegrate irreparably: this, as much as the overt social allegories, is what speaks to an underlying economy.

For that reason–and also because it brings us back to

the geographical location of Fuad Ramses' killing spree – in what remains of this chapter we will be more interested in Romero's third zombie film than those preceding it or those that shamble along in its wake. Released in 1985, *Day of the Dead* spends ample time and spills buckets of guts explaining zombie physiognomy. Set in an underground military base at Fort Myers, Florida, this instalment takes place several years after the zombie apocalypse whose advent was depicted in the first two films. This is a film set after the initial catastrophe. The zombie apocalypse has dawned and we have successfully weathered it out, but only just. An almost overwhelming sense of belatedness coincides with the film's realization after the economic crisis that informed both *The Texas Chain Saw Massacre* and *Dawn of the Dead*. Perhaps it is not coincidental that *Day of the Dead* was made at a time when capitalism temporarily offset its crisis in accumulation by transferring the means of profit-extraction into the field of finance.

Because it is not set during those early stages of the pandemic, this instalment in the zombie cycle affords a slower pace than the previous two entries, within which the undead can be studied scientifically. Hearkening back to the literary terrain on which splatter was inaugurated, the chief scientist at the base, Dr Logan, is known to the other survivors as Dr Frankenstein because of the grotesque surgical vivisections he performs on zombies, which are ostensibly undertaken in pursuit of a way to restore their humanity. In one of the film's more repellent scenes, Logan reveals his discovery that the zombies are driven by an instinctual compulsion to eat. He learns this after having severed the internal organs of one, who when tempted to bite at Logan's fingers sits up on a hospital gurney and spills meaty viscera from an open stomach cavity and onto the floor. "It wants me," Logan explains, before dispatching the zombie by drilling through its forehead. "It wants food! But it has no stomach, can take no nourishment from what it ingests. It's acting on instinct!"

For Marx, human labour is the "metabolic" transformation of natural matter into useful goods, and the ability to labour consciously is what makes humans different from animals, which are driven by sheer instinct. The exploitation of that metabolism under capitalism is what leads Marx to deliver his own array of zombie images: "...by incorporating living labour with their dead substance, the capitalist at the same time converts value, i.e., past, materialised, and dead labour into capital, into value big with value, a live monster that is fruitful and multiplies."[70] When viewed from this perspective, Romero's zombies seem to be analogous to the workforce under capital, so long as that analogy works at a strictly physiological level. The labour undertaken by the zombie is to metabolize living humans into dead meat, turning them either into undead zombies or into food.

Or, if not analogous to the workforce under capital, then the zombies are at least analogous to the workforce in this film, in which scientists labour assiduously at gunpoint to produce "results," using insufficient technology and to a consistently restricted timeline. "You got a little more time," threatens Captain Rhodes, the military figure overseeing this operation. "You got a little more time. A little more, I ain't saying how much. But you better start showing me some results." With injunctions like this, Rhodes presents himself as an archetypal figure of productive capitalism soon to be rejected by neoliberalism, the mid-century manager, whose task was to keep a labour-force on point at all costs. He embodies what a 1973 report on labour famously called "the anachronistic authoritarianism of the workplace."[71] However, this kind of manager was, by the 1980s, being replaced by the neoliberal figure par excellence: the self-sufficient entrepreneur, whom we will meet face-to-face in the subsequent chapter. The social structure of *Day of the Dead* is as economically superannuated as that of the industrial workers in *The Texas Chain Saw Massacre*. But the film seems to know this. The resulting atavism, in which forced labour means the overworked humans and the increasingly sentient zombies begin to resemble one another, is what drives the film towards its bloody apotheosis, when the moving contradiction accelerates production in such a way that the workforce finally implodes through a mixture of psychical collapse and fatal accidents. This, the explosive supersession of a manufacture-based economy, proves nigh on inescapable.

Naturally, the film's bloodiest scene is reserved for Captain Rhodes, that proto-capitalist taskmaster. Whilst attempting to hunt his fleeing workers, Rhodes is gunned down by an exceptionally cognizant zombie before stumbling into a room packed with several of that zombie's undomesticated brethren. After a disjointed series of shot reverse-shots from the perspective of Rhodes, the zombies, and his gun-toting pursuer, Rhodes is shot one last time and dragged down onto his back. The subsequent evisceration is shot from somewhere above Rhodes' right foot. The surrounding zombies all pull in different directions. First legs detach from the torso, which simultaneously splits open, slopping blood and organs across the linoleum. Then, in a shot taken from Rhodes' perspective, we witness his legs being dragged away, trailing a bright red smear. "Choke on 'em!" He gurgles. "Choke on 'em!" What follows is a montage of close-ups and medium close-ups in which the camera follows various limbs and organs, all of which are under mastication. Technically, at the level of shot types and editing, we are once more back with Eisenstein, and as in the films from Lewis and Hooper the exuberant excess of splatter once more attaches itself to that moment when a ruling-class subject is torn apart and made into food. This is the experience of labour in a time of crisis, when the moving contradiction bites down upon its occupants, now turned back against those that seek to exploit their circumstances. It is also the final outmoding of one sociality by another: the apocalyptic onset of neoliberalism.

A Modest Proposal: Eat the Rich!

Let us pause before concluding this chapter and think about the protracted crisis in which these films were created. Lewis' first horror film, Hooper's masterpiece, and Romero's zombie trilogy were all made in that transformative period of American history following the Long Boom after World War II and before the final dissolution of the Soviet Union. This period included an economic crisis whose causes were heralded throughout the 1960s, which erupted as a wholesale collapse in the 1970s, and which lead to a reconstruction of capital throughout the 1980s. While the superstructural reactions to this crisis manifest throughout all our three films – in the foregrounding of immigrant labour, in the narrative centrality of a gas shortage and factory foreclosures, and in the eventual breakdown of managerial hierarchies – what unites these films and their very different narratives is a shared commitment to splatter. They all inhabit the human body's stinking lacunae. By delivering these ultra-violent and outrageously gory films, Lewis, Hooper, and Romero provided the historical coordinates for the first wave of American splatter, before that genre would be commercially superseded during the reestablishment of profitability by different kinds of horror: first by films about haunted spaces and then by the slasher film.

In the background to all three of these films, which all meditate on the exploitation of human labour within the sphere of capitalist accumulation, is not only the signal crisis in American capitalism but also the triumph of the finance sector over the economy as a whole and with that the birth of neoliberalism. The three films all know that despite whatever resolution their narratives offer, the offering is only temporary. The immigrant shop-owner might have been crushed in the garbage compacter, but that doesn't guarantee the end of his insurgency. "So, Frank," speculates one policeman. "Who knows if the spell of this monstrous goddess has possessed anyone else? Lust, murder, food for an ancient goddess who received life through the perverted death of others." Sally escapes the family of cannibals, hitching a ride on the back of a utility truck, but she leaves behind Leatherface, who in the film's final moments spins and twirls with his chainsaw before the amber horizon of a Texan sunrise. He will be back for multiple sequels. The heroes of Romero's third zombie film escape the military base in a helicopter, flying offshore to an apparently uninhabited island in the nearby Bahamas, but no amount of coconut cocktails is going to bring their planet back from this hell (unless, of course, they made it to socialist Cuba!). These endings all know that a crisis has been displaced but not resolved. And when that crisis is displaced, historically, the splatter film seems to go away – or, as we will see in the following chapter, it mutates into something else.

While specific political and historical tensions infiltrate and inform the narratives of these films, such tensions are not necessarily what we are seeing in or as the gore. Rather, those tensions only mediate between capitalist production and the visceral carnage, between the mode of production and an aesthetic of splatter. Looking back to Marx and Eisenstein, we might say that these films capture the horror of productive labour under capitalism, when it has been pressurized by crisis, and that they do so not only in their consciously allegorical narratives. Their scenes of gore, and the visual pleasure those scenes provide, is keyed into a certain kind of utopian wish-fulfilment. That is to say, these films are more than just critical. They provide something other than capitalist realism and they do so with gore. It is tempting here to suggest that these films are optimistic about social transformation. According to horror novelist Michael A. Arnzen, splatter films like these "portray the postmodern condition as an optimistic vehicle for cultural transformation."[72] Optimistic and transformative, maybe, but we should be more specific. It's not the postmodern condition that attracts such hopefulness. Rather, these films only become affirmative when murdering the rulers or eating the rich.

Jean-Jacques Rousseau may have said it best with an eminently quotable aphorism on the back end of the Paris Commune. "When the people shall have nothing more to eat, they will eat the rich." If these films represent the proletariat, or if they cultivate an anti-capitalist populism, that representation and that populism are not about identification with specific characters or actants. We experience visual pleasure not through our identification with the underclass antagonists or with their bourgeois victims, but through the historical process, a way of responding to the crisis that ultimately results in massive bloodshed. There is, to be sure, a dissimulation at work in this. These three films do not exploit some unconscious desire to eat the rich, but rather a more impersonal desire to see the rich eaten, and so in realizing that fantasy they spawn situations wherein the rich are forced to eat themselves. While we have already heard Marx compare the accrual of surplus value to one human "eating the flesh of another," these films ask us to imagine and to really enjoy imagining the corresponding scenario in which the cannibalistic mode of production is forced to cannibalize itself. When the rich begin eating the rich we can sit back and enjoy the show, for our work will be halfway-done. Call it *anthropophagia* of the proletariat.

Third Intermission
Global Ferox

I don't properly remember when or where I first heard about Italian horror. Maybe an IMDB list on a school library computer screen. But this could be a phantom memory. Or maybe it was just a video nasties catalogue. Though I don't know how I first picked up on that one either. Nevertheless, before gaining access to any of the films I had already become fixated on Italy, and in particular on the films directed by Lucio Fulci, Joe D'Amato, Umberto Lenzi, and Ruggero Deodato. I had seen a handful of Dario Argento's more accessible works, but was never really taken with the witchcraft and the black-gloved killers. *Giallo* just wasn't my thing. To my mind, there was an extraordinary exoticism to those other directors, which was at least partially fuelled by the fact that their films were totally banned and so without distribution in Australia. Morbid curiosity thus attached itself to an unreachable set of films whose aesthetic, I imagined not inaccurately, might obtain somewhere between the legacy of Mussolini and a vexed obligation to Catholicism. So deeply scarred and so wracked by guilt, I thought, theirs must have been a horror beyond all comparison.

The first of these films I eventually acquired for screening was the most infamous of all, *Cannibal Holocaust*, which I bought second-hand from an underground record store. The cover featured a badly xeroxed composite image: a human skull, on the forehead of which a band of grass-skirted natives had been superimposed. The design was totemic yet austere, unlike the baroque iconography that first lured me into the world of gore. It suggested something much darker. The man at the counter told me my purchase was "seriously sick shit." He seemed approving. This must have been sometime in the very early 2000s.

Before getting into the film, here are some of the things I did and didn't know from reading about it. I knew that it invented the found footage style of horror, which had just been thoroughly commercialized by *The Blair Witch Project* in 1999. I knew all about the twin sources of its controversy and suspected that both had something to do with the play on verisimilitude. One was that it included the killing of live animals, and the other was that its actors all signed contracts forbidding them from any media appearances for one year following release. The combination of these two factors, actual slaughter and vanished actors, emphasized the realism inherent to found footage, but also triggered a homicide investigation into the director and producers.

What I didn't know is that its director, Ruggero Deodato, had previously worked as production assistant to Roberto Rossellini, and that its verisimilitude should be thought of as an appropriation and extension of neorealism, with that movement's commitment to economic anxiety and class conflict. Truthfully, I had no idea what neorealism was and Rossellini's name meant nothing to me. I didn't know that its footage was modelled on the anti-socialist propaganda films utilized in Italy during the Years of Lead. Similarly, I didn't know about Sergei Eisenstein and his inauguration of a montage that counterpoises the staged killing of humans with the real slaughter of animals. Though I knew its story would cut between New York City and the Amazon, I certainly wasn't cognizant of the double elision taking place in this, which substitutes the United States for Italy and South America for Africa. But even if I had been more sensitive to these substitutions, I likely would not have insisted, as I do now, that rather than amplifying the differences between Italy and the United States, this suggests a meaningful continuity between fascist annexations and democratically sanctioned economic imperialism.

The film's plot comprises two nested stories. In one, an American film crew has disappeared into the Amazon while attempting to shoot a documentary about cannibalism amongst the indigenous tribes. The team comprises Alan Yates, the director; Faye Daniels, his girlfriend and scriptwriter; and their two cameramen, Jack and Mark. The other story is focused on Harold Monroe, an anthropologist from NYU who leads an expedition in hope of recovering the missing filmmakers. Soon after meeting a tribe of natives, Monroe and his guides discover a shrine constructed from the rotting flesh and bones and cameras of the missing filmmakers, set in place "to drive away the evil spirits that the dead represented." The tribe agree to trade the preserved reels of footage for an audio recorder, on which Monroe has captured his own reflections and the voice of their chief. Back in New York, executives from Pan American Broadcasting invite Monroe to host a documentary based on the recovered film. He is shown a mondo film made by the deceased filmmakers on Ugandan war crimes and is told that the footage was all staged, "a put on," and that nobody was harmed in its production. When reviewing the Amazon footage, Monroe is witness to all manner of comparable atrocity dealt out by the filmmakers on the native fauna, both animal and human. A village of natives is burned alive, "just like in Cambodia," which the filmmakers frame as an outcome of tribal warfare. Disgusted, Monroe demands the executives watch two reels of unedited footage that only he has witnessed.

The final two reels begin with the team locating a young native girl, whom the men gang-rape. They later discover the same girl impaled on a wooden pole by a riverbank. "I can't understand the reason for such cruelty," Alan feigns for the camera. "It must have something to do with some obscure sexual rite or with the almost profound respect these primitives have for virginity." The tribe retaliates *en masse*. One cameraman is speared, castrated, and torn to pieces. The viscus is heaved from his limbless torso and consumed. Faye is raped by the native men, then beaten and beheaded by the women. The footage ends with a fallen camera's accidental close-up on Alan's bloody face in the moment of his death. All of this is roughly cut, framed by an unsteady hand, and screened on damaged film stock. It is also punctuated by images of Monroe and the increasingly wide-eyed and disconcerted executives, who will order the footage burned. The film ends with Monroe leaving the station and venturing out into lower Manhattan.

We have already seen American films in which gore precedes the consumption of human flesh. This is a trope that in different film cultures would be worked up into a genre of its own. Specifically, the cannibal film became the most popular sub-sub-genre of splatter in Italy, during the 1970s and 80s, when a handful of opportunistic moviemakers seized upon the critical ethos of neorealism and applied it to spectacles of primitive horror. *Cannibal Holocaust* is archetypal and exemplary of this trend. Indeed, the Italian cannibal films all contain similar elements: found footage; imperialist racism; anthropologists or documentary filmmakers; Amazonian and South East Asian primitivism; animal slaughter; rape; vengeance. If the period that gave birth to this so-called "cannibal boom" belonged to Italy's "economic miracle," its post-fascist reconstruction of capitalism (at the hands of fascists, the neo-fascists, and the heirs of fascism), the means by which that context enters these films is in their positing a relationship of dependency between the modern world and the primitive hearts of darkness. Most frequently of all, as we have already seen, between New York City and the Amazon. Within that relationship, cannibalism serves as an expression of heroic sadism, a force with which the exploited inhabitants of whatever jungle quite literally bite back against their colonizers. When the Amazonian tribespersons mutilate the white adventurers, they do so precisely as an act of retribution, collecting a debt accrued through decades of state-sponsored invasion, rape, murder, and genocide. Those deaths are, in all their ugly viciousness, absolutely and totally satisfying. The eventually and inevitably eviscerated are portrayed as utterly deserving of their fate.

The dynamic of centre and periphery as staged in the cannibal films is familiar to post- and anti-colonial film theory. It was the Brazilian filmmaker Glauber Rocha, a precursor to Third Cinema and the founder of Cinema Novo, who famously explained the anti-imperialist aesthetic as one of blood and hunger. So he writes in his manifesto from 1965, echoing the words of Frantz Fanon:

> We know – since we made those ugly, sad films, those screaming, desperate films in which reason has not always prevailed – that this hunger will not be assuaged by moderate government reforms and that the cloak of technicolor cannot hide, but rather only aggravates, its tumours. Therefore, only a culture of hunger can qualitatively surpass its own structures by undermining and destroying them. The most noble cultural manifestation of hunger is violence.[73]

Of course, films made in post-fascist Italy about imperial relations between the United States and South America technically cannot be Third Cinema. Nevertheless, the aesthetic vision affirmed here is remarkably similar to the neorealist aesthetic exploited in the cannibal films. Economic depredations are met with a violence whose prevailing form, the consumption of human flesh, is in the most literal sense the result of hunger. Gore, from this perspective, acquires a unique revolutionary surcharge, simultaneously redoubling and returning violence from the farthest-flung peripheries of empire, thereby raising an important question for splatter. If the essence of third-world colonialism is indeed horror, what does that mean for the billions living in the first world, and for the American setting of the films with which this book is mostly concerned?

As a filmic trope, cannibalism serves as an atavistic mediator between two seemingly incommensurate realities, taking place simultaneously in the cities of the first world and in the jungles of the third. This is what numerous thinkers have described using the argument, to quote from Ernest Mandel, that "the capitalist world system is to a significant degree precisely a function of the universal validity of the law of unequal and combined development."[74] Indeed, splatter seems to know that first and third worlds are coeval, occupying not only a shared globe or world system but also a shared geographical milieu. *Cannibal Holocaust* reminds us of this with its opening monologue, read by a television presenter over instantly recognizable shots of Manhattan's iconic cityscape:

> Man seems to ignore the fact that on this very planet there are still people living in the Stone Age and practicing cannibalism. Primitive tribes isolated in a ruthless and hostile environment where the prevailing law is the survival of the fittest, and this jungle, which its inhabitants refer to as the Green Inferno, is only a few hours flying time from New York City.

Similarly, the closing shot features Monroe's voiceover as he leaves the television studio: "I wonder who the real cannibals are?" In answer to that question, the shot tracks Monroe as he crosses the street and passes between the Twin Towers of the World Trade Centre, that greatest of all architectural symbols for the violence of globalization, with the camera tilting skyward to emphasize the immensity of their form.

Gore, in this instance, is not just a revolutionary expression of anti-colonialist violence. Not just a blowback from primitive accumulation. It also expresses the uneven and combined development of capitalism.

Perhaps this is why *Cannibal Holocaust*, which stretches a narrative topography between two unevenly developed planes, is so thoroughly preoccupied with analogue media – or, put differently, with the materiality of mediation. From the screening of damaged film footage, through discussions on televisual broadcasting and debates around post-production editing, right down to that exchange of an audio recorder for the reels of lost footage: this is a film as much about the mediation of gore as it is about gore itself, and that might be the entire point. "The moment of violence," says Rocha, "is the moment when the coloniser becomes aware of the existence of the colonised. Only when he is confronted with violence can the coloniser understand, through horror, the strength of the culture he exploits."[75] Though I wasn't thinking this when I first saw *Cannibal Holocaust*, it's impossible not to sense something to the effect of Rocha's words.

I sensed it in the narrative and the bloodshed, of course, but I also sensed it and nowhere more hauntingly than in Riz Ortolanis's accompanying soundtrack, which restages the interaction between colonizer and colonized in the tonal dissonance between acoustic guitars and mawkish strings, on the one hand, and monosynth bass swells and oscillator blips, on the other. It is thus that the score exploits an overwhelming tension between emotive kitsch and impersonal machinery. The soundtrack amplifies the horror of its imagery precisely by refusing to give either the invaders or the invaded privileged access to any one identifying motif, and by charging gore with a politically undetermined electrical field whose sonic drive cuts back through the performed instrumentation and right into the nervous system. Every blow from the invaders' machetes triggers yet another wave of this pulsating retro-futuristic noise, but so does retaliation from the natives. Colonial strife as auditory discord.

Chapter 4

Uncontrollable Organs

Neoliberal Nightmare Bodies

Of all the philosophical ideas that lend themselves to a conversation about splatter, few seem anywhere near so applicable as the "body without organs." This prodigiously expansive concept originated in a radio play by Antonin Artaud, and from there it went on to serve a major role in the middle management infused vocabulary of Gilles Deleuze and Félix Guattari. For those two, the body without organs is a vast many things, reducible to none, but also the result of an economic articulation. In this particularly lucid passage, for instance, it is used to explain the machinations of capitalist enterprise:

> Capital is indeed the body without organs of the capitalist, or rather the capitalist being. But as such, it is not only the fluid and petrified substance of money, for it will give to the sterility of money the form whereby money produces money. It produces surplus value, just as the body without organs reproduces itself, puts forth shoots, and branches out to the farthest corners of the universe.[76]

For Deleuze and Guattari, a being defined by its desire for surplus value is made up of the various organs used to transform money into more money. On the one hand, the skeletal being of capital is an abstract entity whose stratagem is to invest money into commodities to make more money. On the other hand, that being only acquires its qualitative form in the mass of living workers whose muscles, nerves, bones, and brains are grafted onto the body of capital in order to produce value.

Under capitalism, we are all part of this grotesque assemblage – and, for Deleuze and Guattari, the assemblage is mortified by the mechanical brutalization of its living organs. "Every coupling of machines, every production of a machine, every sound of a machine running, becomes unbearable to the body without organs. Beneath its organs," they write, conjuring an image worthy of any director considered in this book, "it senses there are larvae and loathsome worms..."[77] Here, where desire meets with death, the body without organs reads as a Marxist satire on the privileged subject of capitalism, i.e. the capitalist – and, as we shall see, of capitalism when it is operating in one very specific modality.

Though disappointingly less present in the two cinema books by Deleuze, the body without organs is nevertheless alluded to on several occasions, and most explicitly with reference to the ideological force and demystifying potential of Sergei Eisenstein's innovations in film editing. But this has less to do with montage and more to do with lensing human faces in close-up. "The face," we are told, "is this organ-carrying plate of nerves which has sacrificed most of its global mobility and which gathers or expresses in a free way all kinds of tiny local movements which the rest of the body usually keeps hidden."[78] If, as we saw in the previous two chapters, the gore-laden montage is attracted to sites of capitalist industry and of remunerated labour where horror either renders or reverses the violence of exploitation, here we will see how this other side of Eisensteinian style is taken up by splatter cinema in relation to a different kind of capitalist exploitation: how the assimilation of discontinuous organs into the coincidence of a single face responds to the networking imperative of post-industrial, neoliberal capitalism.

"Here," writes Deleuze about Eisenstein, "the intensive series discloses its function, which is to pass from one quality to another, to emerge on to a new quality."[79] Without getting into the subtleties of Deleuzian philosophy, what we will be seeing in this chapter is how film depicts one particular version of the body without organs, when under the dictates of capitalist desire organs are literally dislocated and reassembled into new bodies. Deleuze's emphasis on the face will be just as important to this argument. Whereas the montages we have already seen tend to isolate the traumatized limb or organ, thus giving an almost pornographic emphasis to the gaping orifice, the films we are about to look at target what Deleuze would call the "affection image" or what is readily identifiable as the facial close-up, that sentimentalizing staple of mainstream film aesthetics. Here I want to show that the shift in emphasis – from the depersonalized limb or organ or orifice and the utterly objectified body to the desired or desiring face as the privileged site of horror – is representative of transformations in the economy and of the post-crisis restructuring of labour after the 1970s.

While the previous chapter looked at cannibalism as an emblem of class warfare and as an aggressive response to the signal crisis in capitalist accumulation, this chapter thinks about the way splatter films depict the body without organs in the context of one of capitalism's self-proclaimed victories, which came almost two decades after the displacement of that initial crisis, primarily through finance. On November 9, 1989, the Berlin Wall fell and thus marked the symbolic expiry of state socialism, a chief threat to capitalism's global expansion. The familiar verdict on this historical moment belongs to the conservative democrat Francis Fukuyama, who declared it our arrival at the utopian "end of history," for in 1989 liberal democracy and capitalist enterprise could finally flourish unchecked by their political antithesis: "we have," he insists, "trouble imagining a world that is radically better than our own, or a future that is not essentially democratic and capitalist."[80] What this too easily dismissible diagnosis indicates is the presupposition that, outside of the few socialist states, the entire world was already running on capitalist time.

That Fukuyama made this declaration in the summer of 1989 is just as much a reflection on the decade it concludes as it is on that moment of post-socialist jingoism. Notably, the 1980s had already engineered the eradication of popular anti-capitalist critiques, the likes of which were feeding into the splatter films of the late 1960s and the 1970s. As the sociologists Luc Boltanski and Ève Chiapello demonstrate in their account of the "new spirit of capitalism," or what is increasingly referred to as neoliberalism, the intervallic period between our signal and terminal crises was responsible for "dismantling the world of work," and with that dismantling came the decline of anti-capitalist resistance.[81]

In the wholesale transformation of labour during capitalism's recovery period, work was redefined in terms of versatility and flexibility and autonomy, restructuring principles that disarticulated workers from their class, thereby diminishing the strength of trade unionism while superimposing a newfound precariousness the world over. This situation was concomitant with the dominance of finance over production, but not with production's absolute dissipation. As Joshua Clover explains (with an aptly sci-fi-sounding phrase taken from Derrida):

> Accelerated turnover demands more credit-based liquidity while at the same time expelling labor from production in favor of what we might call process servers: the "techno-telemedia apparatuses" and the administrators of an ever-more-complex-and-hurried command-and-control network, in turn subtended by information-technology and knowledge workers coordinating an increasingly global and futural economic order. Thus, the rise in finance is correlated with the rise of both speculative value and immaterial labor—but this indicates a problem in production, not a new source or mode.[82]

Indeed, labour didn't go away. It evolved. And that evolution gave rise to a new kind of worker and to new kinds of exploitation, operating not just along the familiar class lines but also between individuals: "networkers," write Boltanski and Chiapello,

> succeed in exploiting others by establishing relations with them that can be interpreted in terms of the logic of a domestic world (trust), but in contexts where they can extricate themselves from the forms of control on which the stability of the domestic world was based.[83]

With the rise of neoliberalism, networking became a new form of capitalist enterprise with its own underside of exploitation; and the human face, with all its emotional intensity and its unsurpassed powers of conveyance, its solicitations of sympathetic affection, would thereby replace the muscles, brain, or hands as a principal tool both of labour and of management.

Despite splatter's diminished fortunes in American cinema during the 1980s, it nevertheless enjoyed some small popularity both there and abroad as a particular sub-generic mutation: namely, "body horror." Stuart Gordon best conveys the ethos of body horror with a series of short, convulsive sentences: "Body Horror. Not dead bodies. Your own body. And something is going very wrong. Inside. Your body is betraying you, and since it's your own body, you can't even run away."[84] Realized along these lines, the body without organs presents us with a being made violable by external forces, which overwhelm that body from within and transform it to their own needs.

Of course, body horror's popularity originates not with the horror genre but in fables of far-flung scientific labour, of hard-thinking men and women pushed to the limits of human space. That is what we see in its inaugural manifestation with *The Incredible Melting Man* from 1977, which serves as a bridge between the cannibalistic splatter of the 1970s and the body horror of the subsequent decade. In it, an astronaut is transformed into a gelatinous monster after exposure to a radiation flare off of Saturn and, doubling down on the horror of his own body, he must consume human flesh in order to survive. While this film is justifiably considered one of the worst ever made – mostly due to the fact that, despite its fantastic premise, the execution is just really, really boring – it nevertheless helped wed an aesthetic of splatter with the threat of interstellar pathogens, whose combination would be indispensable to early body horror.

Body horror became exceedingly popular two years later in 1979, when a newly hatched xenomorph burst from John Hurt's chest, entering the world between jets of blood and flapping meat in Ridley Scott's *Alien*. Then, in 1982, John Carpenter's *The Thing* projects the story of several American scientists working in the Antarctic who encounter an ancient shape-shifting alien, which replicates terrestrial life forms but also twists their bodies into insectoid monstrosities defined only by the seemingly infinite malleability of organs.

This film is the very quintessence of body horror. So writes Matthew Pridham, capturing the almost Lovecraftian oddity of its forms: "Every time one of the beleaguered researchers suddenly sprouts new eyeballs or bursts open to reveal fanged mouths and scrabbling limbs, we are confronted by a region almost as alien to us as that of another's mind: our own insides."[85] These three films – *The Incredible Melting Man*, *Alien*, and *The Thing* – collectively advance body horror as splatter's gut-busting successor, or more accurately as its intervallic placeholder.

In what follows, it will be argued that the circuit of capitalist accumulation, which Deleuze and Guattari take from Marx, corresponds to the accumulation of organs into a bodily assemblage behind a face, and to that body's passage through desire and toward death. In short, the visceral detonations of body horror can be viewed as the rending apart of enterprising capitalists from within. Whereas the films we looked at in the previous chapter mobilized a recognizably under- or working-class aggression, the ones we will encounter here are focused more squarely on the networking individual of 1980s capitalism. They satirize with maximum hostility the men and women who have detached from any strong sense of class-consciousness but are nevertheless cashing in on a sociality bent toward upward mobility. In these films, we do not encounter the harsh experience faced by those forced in and out of alienated production. Instead, we encounter the network, a social web dependent upon the production it nevertheless disavows. That is what we are going to see across three films in which bodies without organs respond to the victories of an otherwise crisis-prone capitalism during the 1980s and to capitalism's promotion of the networked individual: first in Canada, then in England, and lastly back in the United States.

Long Live the New Flesh!

David Cronenberg is, as everybody already knows, the director laureate of body horror. During the 1970s and 80s Cronenberg made a series of popular films whose aesthetic consistency was their shared fascination with human bodies mutating and disintegrating in the force of technological and psychical mutagens. Academic film criticism loves Cronenberg, not least because his brand of body horror is so thoroughly and obviously engaged with the exigencies of its moment. "His films," writes Adriana Cavarero,

> insist that the traumatized body cannot be explained simply as a diseased self in need of reintegration with a healthy social public. Instead, the films maintain that mythologies of the self and the nation have *never* been natural, that trauma unmasks alienation, exclusion, and violence that were always part of the everyday exchanges between private and public that the self and the nation depend upon.[86]

Self and nation, but also the economy that inscribes one within the other, which by the 1980s had come to rely in new ways on precisely those exchanges between the psychologized individual and their geopolitical milieu. While we can see how that exchange underwrites body horror in almost all of Cronenberg's early films – finding form in the biomorphic sex-cults, the cloak-and-dagger Consec agents, the psychoplasmatic dwarf-children, not to mention the corporate-sponsored Brundlefly – here I want to settle on his 1983 *chef-d'oeuvre*, *Videodrome*, and say some things about its unique deployment of body horror to figure the new spirit of capitalism.

Set in Toronto, Canada, in the early 1980s, *Videodrome* follows Max Renn, the CEO of a small pornographic television station, Channel 88, who discovers a broadcast signal from Malaysia featuring scenes of extreme violence and torture. Garish snuff: cheaply produced, highly sellable. Layers upon layers of conspiratorial deception unfold as Max uncovers the signal's source and simultaneously loses touch with reality through a series of increasingly bizarre and violent hallucinations. It is soon revealed that the signal is actually broadcast from Pittsburgh, in the United States, and that it is a weapon for the "socio-political battleground in which a war is being fought for control of the minds of the people of North America." To be sure, the signal is owned and broadcast by a NATO weapons manufacturer, the Spectacular Optical Corporation, whose design is to cause malignant brain tumours, which will exact a moral and ideological purge on North America. All the perverts will soon meet their end. Having been exposed to the signal, Max's consciousness starts to break down and, in what may or may not be a state of hallucination, he sets out with his increasingly warped mind and a correspondingly mutated body to hunt down and kill off the moral majority.

To read this film's narrative as an economic allegory is easy enough. The global network of mediated capital flows – forged transnationally between Toronto, Pittsburgh, and Malaysia – speaks to a moment of financial expansion; to a relationship of dependency between the capitalist megalopolis, the gutted steel town, and the disavowed post-colony. While the product itself is made in South East Asia, whereas its consumer base is in Canada and its owners are American, this triumvirate of geographical particulars seems historically significant. Indeed, it was during the 1980s that United States congressional protectionism served first as a lever for opening foreign markets to American goods and services, and it is not without significance here that this geopolitical levering became readily apparent, several years later, with the Free Trade Agreement between Canada and the United States in 1987. Looking to the film's plot, this context hones sharply into view – but it does so perhaps a little too obviously.

This obviousness is the target of an important question in Fredric Jameson's bravura reading of the film's totalizing attempts at cognitive mapping: "Is *Videodrome* not, for example, the story of the classical struggle between a small businessman and entrepreneur and a great faceless corporation?"[87] But there is, of course, so much more to it than this, as Jameson knows:

> So we have here a fairly explicit economic reading of the text as a narrative about business and competition; and it is worth measuring the distance between this overt and explicit commercial content (which most viewers will however take as a secondary pretext for the rest) and that deepest allegorical impulse of all, which insists on grasping this feature as an articulated nightmare

vision of how we as individuals feel within the new multinational world system.[88]

The competition between businesses, between the small-time distributer and the giant multinational, is only the pretext to a more far-reaching attempt to grasp something existential about the historical milieu. The overt and explicit narrative is, in this sense, ancillary to the film's overwhelming sense of existential dread. An anxiety born, on the one hand, of being forced to adapt every aspect of one's social being to the injunctions of the market and, on the other hand, of being on the receiving end of a one-sided class war. It is that feeling, the affective comportment of neoliberal ideology, which this film simultaneously captures and retaliates against with its horror.

Max's first hallucination, which initiates him into the hallucinatory realm of video and which causes the brain tumour, speaks simultaneously to the sex and death drives that attend capitalist desire, and to which splatter has proven itself pre-eminently attuned in its cultivation of visual pleasure. This hallucination also transforms him into the body without organs. Whilst watching a video of his S&M-fixated girlfriend (played by a red-headed Debby Harry of Blondie fame!) in which she murders a TV evangelist, Brian Oblivion, himself a facsimile of the media guru Marshall McLuhan, the television set begins to breathe heavily and to pulsate as though with sexual longing. We are given a close-up on a close-up, an affectionate remediation of the affection-image. How could Max resist? He is drawn toward the television and enveloped by its thick, red lips, crackling with static in all their televisual glory.

From this point on, Max's body begins to mutate by acquiring new, technologically modified organs. Later whilst watching the same television, a massive vaginal cavity opens up on Max's abdomen, into which he inserts and loses a loaded pistol. Later still, he withdraws the pistol from this abdominal holster and it melds with the flesh and sinew of his hand – a handgun. The same ridiculous pun can be observed in his creation of a hand-grenade. Max is his own industry, the synthesis of the worker and its means of production, a self-sufficient monster with infinite potential but propelled forward by the insatiable solicitations of the death drive. The bodily form of neoliberalism's ideal worker.

The film's final act begins when Max meets with Bianca, Oblivion's daughter and successor, who effectively "reprograms" him as an assassin through a series of catechistic repetitions. "You've become the video word made flesh," Max repeats, "I am the video word made flesh," and is given the instruction: "Now that you are the video word made flesh you know what you have to do. You turn against Videodrome. You use the weapons they've given you to destroy them. Death to Videodrome. Long live the New Flesh." It is thus that Max has become an agent of what they call the "New Flesh," an insurgent cell whose principal operation is to annihilate Videodrome. He takes the fight to them, infiltrating a Spectacular Optical tradeshow in Pittsburgh, and hiding in the audience until the CEO and mastermind of the genocide signal, Barry Convex, takes the stage. And here, finally, is the film's climactic affection-image, another yet more disgusting body without organs, rendered as such in Max's assassination of Convex.

"Love comes in at the eye," announces Convex. "The eye is the window of the soul." Upon recognizing Max – now raised from his seat, muscular handgun trained at his target – Convex freezes. The two run back and forth across the stage. Max plugs him with four bullets, three to the abdomen and one to the forehead. Convex goes down, but he doesn't just bleed out. Convex, on the stage floor, is viewed in two shots: first, from an oblique angle, somewhere between a medium shot and a close-up, and then from a close-up, taken from just above his pelvis and looking up toward his chest. His organs come to life and fight their way out of his torso. Animal grunting. Cut to Max, on the microphone: "Death to Videodrome! Long live the New Flesh!" Mic drop. Feedback hiss. Back to Convex, a close-up on his stomach, which is now a gaping chasm of blood and gore with the efflorescence of cancerously yellow-white organs spewing forth.

Then a jump-cut to the facial close-up. The affection-image. Blood pours from the left eye-socket as pupil and retina drift upward into the skull. The brain forces its way through the forehead, which cracks open and takes out the right side of the face with it. All that remains of Convex is a writhing mass of grey cerebral matter as it crowns over an exposed maxilla. Four more shots: the stomach, whose organs are now rearranging themselves as though jostling for distance from the body; the microphone, still hissing with feedback from the stage-floor; an oblique-angle of the bloody mess held together only by its skeleton and a grey flannel suit, with a massive torrent of ichor cascading from beneath the skull; and, finally, one last close-up of the face, taken side-on, its tongue flapping and its brain pulsating. Death to Neoliberalism. Long live the New Flesh.

The Enemy Within: Family Sadism Under Thatcher

Directed by novelist-turned-movie-man Clive Barker and released in 1987, *Hellraiser* delivers one of the grizzliest opening scenes in all of British cinema. First, the libertine Frank Cotton purchases a puzzle box and then, in a dim-lit and empty room, he solves it. The shirtless Frank kneels within a square made of candles, and the camera slowly cranes upward to look down on him from directly overhead, as though the angles want to mimic the movement of his fingers through the puzzle. He manipulates the box, a gold-leafed cube, and it opens up. Blue-white light enters through fractures in the walls and the box emits a bolt of crackling electricity. Frank screams. Three close-ups of hooks piercing rubbery flesh followed by a close-up of his agonized expression.

Several static shots reveal our setting, presumably days or maybe even weeks or months later, leading us from the exterior of a dilapidated mansion; through its doorframe; into a kitchen littered with rotting food; up a stairwell; into a bedroom, in which a single light bulb hangs above a mattress and a cockroach crawls toward a statue of two lovers; up to the attic doorway, on which the camera slowly zooms. The attic has been transformed into a torture chamber. Chunks of flesh are suspended on chains and hooks. Pylons rotate with severed limbs nailed to their wood. Three black-clad figures emerge from the darkness and step across a flooring of viscera: the Cenobites. A hand feels through the bloody mess and reassembles the five pieces of Frank's disaggregated face into a grotesque mask. The film's first affection-image, to be repeated later but in reverse. One of the three figures, a man with nails hammered into his head, collects the puzzle box, closes it, and the house returns to normality.

The film's plot takes place almost entirely within this mansion located somewhere in North London. Frank's American brother, Larry, moves into the inherited property – their childhood home – along with his second wife, Julia, whom we learn via flashback once had an affair with her now mangled brother-in-law. Larry's daughter, Kirsty, lives nearby but refuses to share a roof with her stepmother. When Larry cuts his hand on an exposed nail the blood resurrects Frank but in skinless, zombiefied form, and soon later Julia agrees to harvest men in order to restore her deceased lover, by picking them up in bars and luring them back to the attic, where they are slaughtered. Frank eventually reveals the cause of his condition: having exhausted all sexual and sensory experience, we are told, he sought the puzzle box, a magical device which initiated him into a realm of new and mortally impossible pleasures. In that realm he has been tortured in such a way as to render pleasure and pain truly indistinguishable. Kirsty discovers all of this. Frank murders her father, Larry, and whilst wearing Larry's skin tries to seduce his niece. "Come to Daddy." She leads the Cenobites to Frank and exchanges his life for her own freedom. The film climaxes with Frank, still wearing Larry's skin, being torn apart by hooks and chains and with Kirsty using the puzzle box to vanquish the Cenobites.

What, then, can all of this tell us about its historical moment? The fact that this film contains no reference to history, and barely even glimpses an outside society, is in itself revealing of a social context. 1987 was the year in which neoliberal demon-mother, Margaret Thatcher, was elected for a third term as Prime Minister. Her political legacy was dependent on the very ethos that defined the new spirit of capitalism. So writes David Harvey: "Thatcher forged consent through the cultivation of a middle class that relished the joys of home ownership, private property, individualism, and the liberation of entrepreneurial opportunities."[89] Or, in her own words, the famous Tory axiom: "There is no such thing as society, only individuals." That is what we encounter in *Hellraiser*, whose evidently wealthy characters all subscribe to Thatcherite ideology, whether they know it or not.

Before the film's manifold horrors can unleash themselves on the family, we are introduced to the characters via a discussion of money and of property ownership as decoupled from any kind of familial sentiment. The irony of this introduction is, despite Harry's claim about the inherited mansion that "we'll soon warm it up, make it a proper home," there is absolutely no sense of warmth or homeliness. The mansion is only an asset and he knows this. "I wanted to sell it after the old lady died," says Larry, "but I couldn't get Frank to agree." And, when looking around at Frank's decorations: "Would you look at this! And don't worry. This stuff means nothing to me. It all goes." Society is mediated exclusively by private property and its market value.

This clear sense of a society shorn to nothing by the profit nexus extends into almost every aspect of the film's narrative. As Patricia Allmer has argued in a detailed summary that bears lengthy quotation:

> We find out nothing about Larry's job except that it is 'terrific'; we never find out about his first wife, Kirsty's mother; we never find out where the family came from, nor is there much indication in the film of where the house is actually located. Conflations between English buildings and streets and American accents further obscure the location of the characters and enforce the atmosphere of isolation, displacement and homelessness that lies at the heart of the film's exploration of the ideology of home ownership: the house they move into looks like an old English Victorian mansion, curiously inherited by the American Larry and his English wife and American daughter; the removal men are American, but the businessmen Julia tempts to the house are English. Individuals exist here, but only as actants, devoid of character or depth, suggesting a world in which even individualism has collapsed in upon itself.[90]

More than any of these details, however, what locates the

film within its historical situation is an overwhelming lack of human warmth, which translates most palpably into the film's striking deficiency of sexual charisma despite its rampant sexuality. This is a nightmare vision entirely devoid of passion. For instance, the flashback sequence to Frank and Julia's affair is jarringly vanilla. Frank, a pleasure-seeker on the order of the Marquis de Sade's infamous libertines, a man whose desire transcends the mortal realm in its entirety, commits himself to just a few moments of tasteful missionary in soft rom-com lighting. While sex was a principal commodity in *Videodrome*, there it was still depicted as erotic. Despite or even because of their circumstances, those characters really wanted to fuck, and the film exploited that. In *Hellraiser*, by contrast, the reification of desire is complete. This is more than a queer writer and director's despairing take on the cult of heterosexual boredom. Rather, despair inheres within the fact that sex has become purely instrumental – that, as we shall see in a moment, it exists primarily to establish networks between individuals.

First, however, we must account for the film's body without organs, a creature made animate by outdated stop-motion. When Larry slices his hand on an exposed nail the camera cuts to an extreme close-up of the blood splashing on the attic's wooden floorboards, captured in slow motion, before it is rapidly absorbed into the cracks. The camera then descends into the floor itself under which, surrounded by cobwebs, a suspended heart begins to pulsate. After Larry is taken to hospital for stitches, the camera returns us to the attic, moving slowly – as though intrepidly – and accompanied by a gradually amplifying score pitched somewhere between a waltz and fairground music. The floorboards lift and shudder. A gelatinous liquid wells up from nail-holes. Two long, insect limbs spring upward and drag a mucus-coated form out of this growing pool of liquid matter. A quivering brain congeals itself out of pink goo and the skeletal form plants itself into the cerebellum. Digits extend themselves worm-like to fulfil hands and feet. Entrails are siphoned up into a rib cage. The camera pulls back for a medium-shot: backlit by shafts of sunlight the figure, a skeleton surrounded by exposed organs, looks upward and groans. The mansion's rightful owner has returned.

After this initial congelation, the skinless body without organs – which is, of course, a resurrected Frank – continues to grow in strength by drinking the blood of other men. I want to suggest that it is in the execution of this plot that our film embraces the fully realized horror of networking. The middle part of the film features multiple scenes of Julia visiting an over-lit cocktail bar and picking up suited, day-drinking strangers whom she takes home, where they are expeditiously murdered so that Frank may ingest their flesh and blood. "See, it's making me whole again," he tells her, after consuming the first victim. "Every drop of blood you spill puts more flesh on my bones, and we both want that, don't we?" Predictably enough, Frank is using the affair to exploit Julia, and as he acquires human features he becomes all the more capable of doing so, not least because he transforms from the skinless monstrosity into a figure capable of conveying, with his fully-formed face, affective intensity. His resurrection is completed in the murder of Larry, his brother, whose face he adopts as a skin-mask, and then with the murder of Julia. "Nothing personal, babe." This is capitalist accumulation in the age of networking.

Given this film's emphasis on individualism, and on networking, small wonder that its bloody apotheosis takes the form of an affection-image, the facial close-up. After Frank chases Kirsty into the attic – where she stumbles across the flayed corpse of her father – the attic once again transforms itself into that torture chamber known to us from the opening scene. Hooks and chains from wall to wall. The Cenobites return. "This isn't for your eyes," Pinhead instructs Kirsty. Again, Frank is attacked by hooks and chains, which pierce and pull his skin in every direction, stretching flesh and membrane far from his skull. We are finally given a close-up of his face, and the horror is in its detail, in how irreparably damaged that face has become: inked in blood from where the skin has torn free from its scalp; one cheek is gouged wide open; and both cheeks are dragged outward in such a way that the left eye is nothing more than a horizontal slit. It looks excruciating, and is positively disgusting to behold. Frank slowly, lasciviously licks his lips and draws out his final words. Three unbearably long syllables. A drawl: "Jee-zzuus wept." He really is the creepiest of creepy uncles. The scene cuts to Kirsty then back to Frank, viewed over Kirsty's shoulder, as his body is pulled apart with so much force as to explode it into numerously unrecognizable chunks of flesh.

Rendezvous With Destiny: Beverly Hills Blood Orgy

While *Videodrome* and *Hellraiser* both feature the migration of American capitalist values into geopolitical elsewheres – through a global network that links Canada and Malaysia via Pittsburgh, and through an American family's emigration to Thatcherite England – for this chapter's final offering we return to American soil for the deliriously stomach-churning satire on class segregation, *Society*, which was completed in 1989 but only released in 1992. This film presents an insider's view on the beneficiaries of Reagan-era capitalism. Its plot is about an ostensibly highborn young man, Bill Whitney, and his attempts to navigate the ruling-class establishment of Beverly Hills despite growing suspicions of his family's implication in some unspoken, underlying horror. "I feel like something's gonna happen," he tells his psychiatrist in the opening scene. "And if I scratch the surface there'll be something terrible underneath it."

That sense of doom is fuelled by fleeting moments of uncanny recognition that could just as easily be mistaken for the desire-addled projections of a horny teenager. There is something almost Lynchian to this. First, Bill sees the flesh on his sister's back perspire then pulsate, as though there is an alien something living beneath it. Second, he spies on his sister through a shower screen and it looks as though her abdomen faces the wrong direction, ass-forward. And later, a sexual partner's limbs appear in all the wrong places and facing all the wrong directions, like a dislocating glimpse of kama-sutric sex taken way too far. That these visions might be hallucinations is effectively disproven when Bill is given an audio recording by his sister's ex-boyfriend, Blanchard, whom we will meet again. On it, mother, father, and sister can be heard arriving at the sister's debutante ball. "Remember the schedule," says their father. "First we dine, then copulation. Someone your own age first. Then your mother and me. Then in comes the host." After discussion of coupling and of breast-size the mother reassures her anxious though excitable daughter: "It's fun to see how far you can stretch. The hotter and wetter you get the more you can do. It's great!" The recording finishes up with female moans and male screaming. An acousmatic grab of what we suspect the ruling class get up to behind closed doors.

Of course, the saturnalian metaphor of capitalism-as-orgy dates as far back as Balzac, for whom the nobles' orgy served as the horizon of suicidal desire and as a fantastical counterpoint to the harshness of its own subtending realities, and it reaches something like its literary pinnacle with Thomas Pynchon, in whose epic the wartime Europeans fuck their way to an immanent though inescapable mass death. But the late-80s presented an opportunity like no other for capital, as Marx once phrased it, to celebrate its orgies. While tight monetarist policy was the first constituent of neoliberalism under Ronald Reagan – curing post-1970s inflation by raising interest rates, which in turn lead to higher unemployment rates and to the destruction of organized labour – that policy was flanked by the administration's infamous advocacy of supply-side or "trickle-down" economics. Tax cuts for the super-rich – in the top bracket, from 70 percent down to 28 percent – accompanied by an increase in payroll taxation, targeting the working class.

In a sense, this is what Fukuyama announced. He was nothing if not a hype man for neoliberalism, the celebrant of its orgy, in which Reagan and Thatcher committed themselves to the most vigorous rutting. So reflect Zygmunt Bauman and Stanislaw Obirek, with an emphasis on the accompanying shift to a finance economy:

Reagan/Thatcher's thirty-year long orgy of consumption, made possible by life on credit and the spending of unearned money masking the unpleasant and potentially explosive effects of persistently rising social inequality and the growing vulnerability of the foundations on which the habitual optimism and self-confidence of the middle-class rested, brought about a brutally bitter awaking; to this day, dazed and confused, we cannot fully shake off the effects of the hangover.[91]

And yet, as history teaches us, that moment of triumph was destined for crisis. "In the middle of the revelries," quipped Jean Baudrillard as early as 1990, "a man whispers into the woman's ear: What are you doing after the orgy?"[92] What this film, *Society*, does is stage the depraved hedonism of the ruling class immediately before the inevitable decline into a skull-crushing hangover. That decline's inevitability was felt as a powerful anxiety after the massive financial disturbance of Black Monday in 1987. While the market's rapid recovery through the intervention of the Federal Reserve – headed by Alan Greenspan – helped conjure away that anxiety, for the American ruling class of the late-80s it once again made clear that sustained economic power would require a firm political base in Washington. Come 1990, the Treasury would insist that the key role of the state needed to be one of "failure containment" rather than "failure prevention." It is thus that the neoliberal imperative of networking finds itself renewed in the necessity for plutocracy. The capitalists needed more than ever to befriend politicians – and what better way to make friends than invite them to your orgy.

That imperative is given full run in the film's finale, when the conspiracy of an orgiastic ruling class comes together, confirming Bill's suspicions and then some, at an establishment party in celebration of the heretofore Washington-based grandee, Judge Carter. Bill, having been captured and dragged through the palatial mansion in bondage, is treated to the kind of pre-victory confessions typical of James Bond movies. It is revealed that, as we should have supposed all along, Bill is not one of them. "A different race from us, a different species, a different class," we are told, because he was not "born into society." The guests undress in nervy excitement, presumably in anticipation of yet another bacchanalia. The dialogue reflects the interpenetration of sexual anticipation with networking enterprise. "We may have an internship for you this summer in Washington," says Judge Carter whilst stripping down and lighting up a cigar. Again, as in the previous two films, sexual desire acts as a medium for capitalist accumulation.

But, once again, the desire proper to capitalism is presented as utterly horrific. So horrific, in fact, that it's difficult to describe what happens next.

Blanchard, the sister's ex-boyfriend that gifted Bill with the audio recordings, is delivered to the front door and brought in, also in bondage. A waltz plays and the black-tie establishment tear Blanchard's clothes from his body and begin rubbing and sucking at the exposed flesh. Everyone is inexplicably lubed up in a viscous ectoplasmic goo. Limbs begin warping together, so that mouths become suction funnels; muscles are made gelatinous; and fingers sink deep into an assuaged rump. "Didn't you know, Billy Boy," someone tells our hero, "the rich have always sucked off low class shit like you." Judge Carter, now in boxer shorts and a singlet, is tasked with performing the *coup de grâce* on Blanchard. "He's good and pliable, your honour," announces a voice from the puddle. "Look! Look! A beauty mark!" Judge Carter delights in chewing off and absorbing that physiological sign of identity, a marker of the face's singularity. "And now," he delivers a Cronenberg-esque pun, "we'll get to the bottom of this." Drumroll. Judge Carter fists Blanchard. We see the outline of his hand through Blanchard's now-pliable chest as it works its way upward to eventually explode from the victim's mouth and grab hold of his face, which is pulled outward and away from the skull.

Bill is chased through the mansion to upstairs, where he finds his amalgamated parents and sister. His father's face emerging from the asshole of his wife, Billy's supposed mother, and his sister's face from that same woman's crotch. Like an Escher painting made of flesh. He flees back downstairs, to the less familial orgy. The music changes again: no longer a waltz but, now, something like broken carnival music. The orgy is barely recognizable as human: just a tremulous mountain of limbs and flesh, fellating and fucking and cannibalizing itself, pouring champagne into and smoking cigars with whatever openings are present. More horror in the details: someone sucks out a loosened eyeball; a mammary dangles freely overhead; a woman drops clumps of long hair into her mouth. It is, in Mark Kermode's spellbound description, "a pulsating mass of shuddering, undulating orgiastic meat with outcrops of recognizable human features – an arm here, a head there, and way over yonder something vaguely resembling an anus."[93] This, to be sure, is the film's lurid vision of neoliberal society: the fully realized capitalist network, a glutinous assemblage of bodies without organs.

Bill is brought to the centre of all this. He challenges one of the society members. "Well well," announces another, paused from sucking the meat out of Blanchard's foot, "a slave revolt." Judge Carter emerges from the puddle to commentate the final showdown – between Ted "The Tycoon" Ferguson and Bill "The Bastard" Whitney – but only after vomiting up a clump of hair. The scene plays out like a typical movie fight but with red lighting and before a cheering crowd of semi-naked millionaires. Bill takes a beating. Ted, assuming he is victorious, kisses his adversary on the mouth. Sucking sounds. But, when Ted tries to fist his opponent Bill grabs his hand and twists it back upon itself. Bill then delivers what Vladimir Lenin once called a "fist from below." Ted pulls away, his face stretched out into a something like a duck's bill, and a weirdly cartoonish sound-effect, a kind of bodily vibrato, concretizes that utterly unreal image. The face springs back to shape, just in time for Bill's thumb to emerge from its mouth. All of what follows is in close-up: index and middle finger poke out the eyes, which fall away with clumps of brown meat clinging to their rear. The three fingers close together collapsing the face in upon itself, before pulling the head down through the collarbone and out through the sphincter, leaving a mass of worm-infested flesh. "Don't touch it 'til he's congealed," shouts one partygoer. As with the other two films, *Society* culminates in the annihilation of the capitalist's face, the revelation of its revolting organs, as though the film itself wants to lay siege to the very embodiment of neoliberalism. And, once again, that annihilation is deployed as an affection-image, the close-up on a face in its moment of omphalic unbecoming.

Peeling Back the Great Ephemeral Skin

This chapter began with Deleuze and Guattari, with their description of the simultaneously desirous and cadaverous body of capital, and with the transposition of that concept into film form, via the affection-image or facial close-up, which warps bodies as though by montage to combine flesh and flesh and face and face. In all three of these films, capitalist accumulation via networking is shown as fittingly libidinal – in the pornography of Chanel 88, in the lasciviousness of libertine Frank, and in mind-bendingly grotesque orgies. As such, the film's presentation of the new spirit of capitalism is as much the presentation of a libidinal economy as anything else.

These films formalize what Jean-François Lyotard seemed to be implying when he likened the material conditions of late capitalism to "the great ephemeral skin."[94] Neoliberalism is the ideological membrane that holds it all together. The epidermis that keeps the meat and bones and organs working together as one. And yet, in their privileging of the affection-image, a close-up of the capitalist's face in the moment of its devastation, these films also satirize the beneficiaries of that economy. They peel back the skin. And behind every face, no matter how successful, is an infinite abyss of writhing organic matter, of "larvae and loathsome worms," whose vitality outlives the body by which it is bound. Behind this membrane is the same festering suppuration that had been there all along.

That shared tendency, the mortification of desire and of its outward form, is readily apparent elsewhere across the globe in contemporaneous body horror films. Perhaps most notable is the Japanese film, *Tetsuo: Iron Man*, released in 1989. This black-and-white cyberpunk fever-dream is forged from the same stuff as David Lynch's *Eraserhead* and shares DNA with its anime namesake from *Akira* (1988). In it, an industrial machinist is struck down and killed by the car of a wealthy businessman, whose body soon begins a muscle-rending metamorphosis into a walking pile of scrap metal. This transmutation inflicts itself upon the businessman's sexuality: he dreams that his girlfriend rapes him with a snaking metal probe, before he awakens to impale her with his phallus, which has evolved into an industrial power drill. Moreover, if the neoliberal ideology to which body horror responds reaches its apotheosis in 1989 with the fall of the Berlin Wall, it is there, in West Germany, that body horror films are at their harshest in pushing desire toward death.

Possession, released in 1981, uses Cold War espionage as a backdrop to its glimpse into a family's catastrophic end, as a young mother nurtures a cephalopodic beast into sexual maturity. Or, shifting out of body horror into a bleaker and more nauseating shade of splatter, the two *Nekromantik* films –1987 and 1991, from either side of the fall –explore the twisted psychosexual life of a nation scarred by Nazism and cleft in two by geopolitical superpowers. Theirs is a morbidity unmatched anywhere save for the unflinching nihilism of the torture porn flicks we will encounter in the following chapter.

Using the body without organs as a figure for capitalist accumulation does not belong to Deleuze and Guattari. Rather, this figure has its origins in Marx, who knew that capital is indeed dead until integrated with living life forms, at which point it acquires tremendous productive power and is born anew. This is how Marx describes that rebirth, in one of the most memorable images he ever produced, a harrowing figure of industrial production, the very apex of capitalist modernity:

> Here we have, in the place of the isolated machine, a mechanical monster whose body fills whole factories, and whose demon power, at first veiled under the slow and measured motions of his giant limbs, at length breaks out into the fast and furious whirl of his countless working organs.[95]

This is not just the means of industrial production, a factory full of dead machines; it is the forces of production, a factory filled with dead machines sucking life from an attendant army of labourers, that system's "countless working organs." Capitalism is, for Marx as much as it is for Deleuze and Guattari, a body teeming with organs. The difference between Marx's account of capitalist organisms and what we have encountered in this chapter, both in that Deleuzian trope and in the films themselves, is a neoliberal inversion of industrial manufacture: here and now the working class has been remade as a network of individuals, and a network historically destined for its own terminal crisis, which would strike with a vengeance in the first decade of the twenty-first century.

While that crisis looms large on the horizon of these films, all of which culminate in the mortification of capitalist desire and the destruction of the capitalist body, here we can conclude that, in this protracted though transient moment of neoliberal triumph, gore films not only provided stories of insurgency, as they did in the 1960s and 70s, but they also satirized the victorious class and its social logic. As we have seen it here, the body without organs and its formalization into splatter serves as a grotesque caricature of neoliberalism. It points up the horror that inhabits the willingly networked individual. May he or she rot from within.

Fourth Intermission

Klaatu Barada... Necktie

A camera emerges from thick, swirling fog, ducks a fallen branch, and leaps another. It flies just a few inches above murky water. Grey sky. Autumnal. Late afternoon. Dead leaves falling from blackened trees. Reflections on the surface. The camera cranes upward, over a branch, and swoops back down to the water, swinging right then left. The movements are fluid and vertiginous. They suggest embodied perspective. A living presence. The shot suffers from the slight distortion of a wide-angle lens. It suggests sight. On the soundtrack a low, inhuman voice gurgles and growls. Is that a submerged car? Too late. Next shot. A yellow Oldsmobile pulls along a ridgeway accompanied by the sound of a woman singing. We see it from the thing's viewpoint. The shot pans to follow, from left to right. Now we're in the Oldsmobile. The song belongs to the driver and his girlfriend. It's just a little too sweet, too wholesome. Their harmonies are almost too perfect. But these two are not the only passengers in the car. Three more in the backseat. Two women, one man. He looks straight into the camera and makes a goofy face. Cut back to the thing's perspective. Whatever it is, it has left the pond and races through the woods. The movements are much, much faster now but nowhere near as fluid. Sounds of metallic reverberation. And its voices, no longer one but multiple, form an inhuman counterpoint to that too wholesome singing and its too sweet harmonies. Cresting a hilltop, the thing screams. So begins what has been for almost two decades my favourite horror film. It's a perfectly menacing sequence. What I skipped in its description is the title, which reflects on the water's surface just as the fog begins to clear. In shimmering blood-red letters: THE EVIL DEAD. This film, the directorial debut for Sam Raimi, was first released in 1981 and became one of the official video nasties. Nevertheless, it was easily accessible in Australia and so I saw it early.

The plot is simple enough. Five students from Michigan State University travel into the Tennessee hills to a small, secluded cabin: the original cabin in the woods. In the cabin's basement they find the *Naturom Demonto*, an ancient book of funerary rites and incantations, "bound in human flesh and inked in human blood," along with tape-recorded recitations from it. The recordings awaken a demonic presence in the woods. One by one the students succumb to the demon and are swiftly transformed into Deadites: zombie-like agents of both mischief and murder. The last to submit, the film's only survivor, is Ash (he was the male passenger, the one that looked goofily into the camera). During the film's second half, Ash is forced to dismember his three possessed friends and his possessed girlfriend, hacking them apart with a dagger, axe, and shovel, blasting at them with a double-barrel shotgun, and gouging out his male friend's eyes. Despite its abundant supernaturalism, this is most definitely a splatter film. The deaths are all excessively gory. Ash's hard-won victory comes when the cursed book falls into the fireplace and, as it burns, the Deadites decompose into a festering mess of meat and bones, teaming with worms and cockroaches. Ash, slaked head-to-toe in blood, limps out into a sunrise soundtracked by saccharine strings and twee birdsong. But, in a final shot, that thing from the opening scene awakens once more, flies down the hill, bursts through the cabin, and descends upon our hero. He turns and screams, with the thing aimed straight into his open mouth. And with that the film cuts to its end credits.

The love of any given film is always going to be a highly personal affair, bound up in biography as much as it has to do with the film itself. My affection here is no exception. I first watched this one at my grandparents' house on a Friday night, the school week over. It was accompanied by pizza and fizzy drink. Their television was a grey box with no remote controller: instead you changed channel by pressing big, square buttons on its base; the volume and picture were controlled by two round knobs. The video recorder was of a similar ilk. Nostalgia for that setting is always present when I watch the film again – something I have done so many times as to lose count over the years – as is the initial excitement of seeing the black cassette disappear into the machine. Part of me regrets that, for whatever reason, I just can't recall the coming attraction trailers that would have accompanied this one.

Nevertheless, there's plenty to love about this film from a technical standpoint, not least of which is its utterly unique sense of visual style: the way that it has a very distinct personality of its own, unlike anything else you will ever see. Its idiosyncrasies and inventions are manifold. These include the camera's ominous and embodied roaming through the woods, the motorcycle-mounted shaky-cam, the charged dynamism of dead space within almost any given shot, the pregnant significance of extreme close-ups, the truly disconcerting use of silence, the gallons upon gallons of syrupy blood, and the retrograde stop-motion employed for the Deadites' ultimate meltdown. Horror had never looked like this before, and it hasn't since.

Most emblematic of this distinctiveness is a scene late in the film when all of its technical flamboyance combines into a reflection upon itself and its status as splatter. Ash ventures down into the cabin's basement to find that even the architecture has turned against him. A pipe explodes, spraying him with a torrent of gore. Two power sockets ooze blood. A single light globe fills with the same crimson goo. And, finally, the old cinematic technologies come to life: a phonograph and a film projector turn themselves on. Ash stumbles about, blinded by the projector's light, and to the sound of a jazz traditional that would be more appropriate behind Buster Keaton than Bruce Campbell. For just a few seconds here a gore-drenched, shotgun-toting Ash seems trapped inside a film-within-a-film. Blood drips onto the projector's magnifier and from top to bottom the whole shot turns red. In the remediated projection of blood on blood, the gore itself seems to have edged toward self-consciousness, as though it too has become possessed by some demonic intelligence. The film seems to know just how gloriously excessive it really is.

As Philip Brophy says of horror in general: "the pleasure of the text is, in fact, getting the shit scared out of you – and loving it, an exchange mediated by adrenalin."[96] For me, this has always been truer of splatter than of any other kind of horror. Gore films are simply the most fun. And, if I were to pin that belief on any one film, this one would be it. Perhaps this is why I was so disappointed to discover that, by the time I first encountered him in the mid-1990s, Sam Raimi had stopped making horror movies. After Ash returned to the cabin for the 1987 sequel, which was really more of a remake, and after he fought off the Deadites once and for all in a time-travelling, medieval adventure from 1992, Raimi relinquished the franchise and went on to direct a spate of commercially successful though totally anodyne genre flicks. To be sure, it's not that I thought he sold out that bothered me. It's that his aesthetic – with its Harryhausen-esque blend of stop-motion, claymation, and practical effects – seemed to have completely disappeared from the cinematic landscape, finding its inadequate heir in the soulless algebra of CGI. My disappointment, however, was transitory, because Raimi wasn't done with gore. Indeed, he would make a triumphant return to splatter in 2009 with *Drag Me to Hell*, which redeploys almost all of the techniques that made *The Evil Dead* so unique.

At its narrative core, *Drag Me to Hell* is about a housing eviction. It focuses on an elderly gypsy woman forced from her home by Christine, the bank's pathologically aspirational loan officer. After pleading unsuccessfully for an extension on her mortgage payment, after falling to her knees and begging, the woman condemns Christine with an ancient curse. Unless Christine passes that curse to another deserving victim, she will be tormented for three days by an evil demon, the Lamia, which will then drag her into the fiery depths of hell where she will suffer for all eternity. At the same time as devising this suitable and fair punishment for bankers the world over, this film taps into another crisis in capitalist accumulation. Just as so much of the gore we have seen articulates the crises of the 1970s and the recovery period of the 1980s, *Drag Me to Hell* locates itself in the first decades of the twenty-first century, and in particular against the mortgage-defaults that would ultimately trigger the global financial crisis.

What combines this film's social knowledge with its self-conscious realization of splatter is that the gore itself undertakes much of the allegorical labour. Specifically, the film's obscene cornucopia of bodily liquids affords us an extended meditation on financial liquidity. The film's protagonists and antagonists are united not only by the insoluble chains of credit and debt – metaphorized as a curse – but also in the fact that their bodies all spew the same cascading torrents of revolting death fluid. Everybody in this film's emphatically credit-based economy is inescapably liquefiable, and this liquefaction is utterly contagious. This interpretation is not original to me. Rather, it belongs to

Annie McClanahan, whose brilliant essay locates the film within a failing finance economy, wherein profits derive from accrued debt and from the liquefaction of assets. In McClanahan's estimation,

> the formal mechanisms of suspense become an index of the somatic tolls of risk; the visual excesses of gore are now the signs of financial contagion and toxicity. Like the characterization of complex financial derivatives as 'Frankenstein's monsters,' Raimi's film draws on the traditions of horror to describe a new kind of terror – the deadliness of financialized debt and credit crisis.[97]

Here, as in so many other splatter films, gore not only coincides with but also results from and therefore materializes before our eyes the potentially intangible vicissitudes of the market.

This is a film whose personal significance is no less dramatic than the director's offering from almost three decades earlier. Specifically, it was in seeing this film that I first became aware of the relationships between splatter and capitalism, between gore and the economy. I'm tempted to say this is because, in 2009, I was no longer a dopey adolescent obsessively trying to screen every horror film I could access; but, truthfully, I was still that person: just as dopey and obsessive, only a little older and with a tertiary education's worth of reading under my hat. The real reason this film would resonate in the way it did is the historical moment during which I saw it. My childhood was in the 1990s, which means I never lived through the crises of the 1970s or the neoliberal recuperation of the 1980s. Even though Australia remains relatively untouched by the economic meltdown, the global financial crisis was an awakening of sorts, in that it pushed the depredations of capitalism and the structuration of value into full view for anyone who cared to look, and made savagely clear that you too are a part of this.

I had read a good deal of anti-capitalist theory and had joined the socialist group at university, but it was not until the global financial crises that I realized my own family's existence had always been indexical to the abstract and incomprehensible fluctuations of the market. Political economy was something I had thought but not felt, or at least not directly. But to read or watch the news in 2008 and 2009 was to be reminded that you and everyone you care about could very easily go under.

While my family had always been on the wrong side of that all too legible divide between the working and the middle class, the idea of an economic downturn had not, until this point, registered as a source of personal anxiety. But this time it did, which was only worsened by the fact that Australia's elected governments had, in my lifetime, been either far- or central-right, articulating a state that would foreseeably follow the US in bailing out its banks with public money and the UK in implementing austerity measures. Within this climate of fear, ours was the kind of remunerated work that either disappears altogether or whose conditions of reproduction transform from bad to worse. I had just spent several years paying rent through variously shitty contracts – house painter, office drone, elementary school drama teacher, barista, and even a short stint on the graveyard shift in a local sex shop – but as of 2009 I had entered graduate school and so could finally live from a university stipend. Dad was a security guard becoming increasingly reliant on public provision, first with healthcare and then, once he couldn't work any longer for precisely the reason he needed healthcare, on a pension. Mom shuttled between multiple low-end retail jobs. Hardly coal mining, but not exactly secure, either. To spend one's lifespan labouring under various kinds of exploitation and to little or no reward went, in the space of months, from being just the way things are to being affectively dreadful.

I share this information not as a tiresome complaint and definitely not to overstate what really is an unexceptional state of precariousness but, rather, to explain why Raimi's homecoming to gore struck me as revelatory. If our taste in film is personal, so too are our political commitments, insofar as any ideology, no matter how collectivist it claims to be, must first speak compellingly to something within a living consciousness and must do so under real social conditions. This is what the philosopher Alain Badiou, whose books I was reading at the time, describes as the subjective process of politicization. "Even in our personal lives, there must be an encounter, there must be something which cannot be calculated, predicted or managed, there must be a break based only on chance."[98] It was around this time, when my political commitments were solidifying into what they are today, that Raimi's film told a story about capitalism that seemed both ideologically and personally compelling, and which utilized a visual language I had come to love many years earlier. I had always known that, in Raimi's films, gore had a mind of its own. This time, however, I also knew what it was thinking.

Chapter 5
Spectacular Torture

Terminal Crisis: A Model Based on Fear

Open to an iris shot of what looks like a disused basement. Dim lighting reveals a trestle covered with crude surgical equipment. Muffled breathing. A man enters the room wearing a procedure mask and butcher's apron. Cut to a young, shirtless man as the black sack through which we were seeing things is lifted from his face. "What? Who are you? Where the fuck am I? What the fuck is this shit?" Shots of the surgical equipment and of handcuffs binding him to a metal chair. The surgeon-butcher returns with a power drill, pumps its trigger, and plunges it deep into his victim's thigh. More screaming. Extreme close-up on the drill's penetration. Yes, it's supposed to be this homoerotic. A shot of the tool bench, to which the drill is restored with chunks of flesh spiralled around its bit. The torturer once again returns to his victim, who is now bleeding from multiple punctures and is covered in his own vomit, and holds up a scalpel. "I always wanted to be a surgeon," he claims, before showing that the tremors in his hands prevented that. "So I went into business. But business is so boring. You buy things you sell them. You make money you spend money. What kind of life is that?" More crying. "You want to go? Is that what you want?" He disappears from view, the young man's screaming intensifies over two impossibly loud slashing sounds, the handcuffs are removed, and a door opened. "You are free to go." The young man attempts an exit and buckles over before he can stand: we are shown in close-up that his ankles have been sliced open, straight across the tendons. He collapses under his own weight.

Having endured this unforgivingly sadistic scene from Eli

Roth's 2005 *Hostel*, we now find ourselves in the "emotional state" that helped usher in the global financial crisis during the first decades of the twenty-first century. Or at least that is what we would have been taught if we were the undergraduate students of free market evangelist, Luigi Zingales, at the Chicago Business School. To test the hypothesis that the crisis resulted not from structural contradiction but from fearful investors withdrawing funds out of the exchange market and thereby causing a sharp decrease in stock prices, Zinagales and his colleagues asked their students a series of questions about risk, but only after exposing a random sample of those students to the kind of footage we have just encountered. "The maintained assumption in this experiment," they would later reflect, "is that the fear generated by the horror movie in the lab acts in a similar way as the fear activated by watching the news about the financial crisis."[99] Collapsing the distance between financial abstraction and destructible bodies, to see stock prices plummet is apparently akin to witnessing scenes of torture. Indeed, it is said that the students who witnessed the footage became more risk averse, leading Zingales to conclude that the behaviour of investors at the onset of the global financial crisis was conditioned by dread, terror, and anxiety, which for him invites further research into "the trading implications of a model based on fear."[100]

Irrespective of Zingales' intentions or the experiment's reported outcome, much of which speaks to the worst kind of libertarian humanism, what the experiment nevertheless betrays is an unconscious awareness of the financial market's irreducible materiality and that materiality's coherence with horror. That Zingales elected to screen a splatter film instead of something supernatural – which might have been more appropriate, given that recent ghost films tend to feature more startling jump-scares, not to mention the neat parallel between haunted houses and home evictions – suggests a potential association between bodily destruction and the apparently abstracted vicissitudes of the financial market. But the association is more than just emotional or reactive. There is an analogical fit between the two, with the intersection of living human bodies and what the scene describes as the "boring" life of business. That intersection plays out in the structuration of the economy itself. Finance is dangerous not because it provides the opportunity for Fortune 500 companies and billionaire investors to rip one another off. Finance is dangerous because, somewhere further down the line, the racketeering folly of those companies and their investors will lead to destitution, destruction, and death, when the crisis-prone market sinks its teeth not only into industry, which is sent offshore and its workers fated to harsher conditions than ever, but also locally when it devours housing, healthcare, education, and pensions.

As we have seen in the background of the previous two chapters, the signal crisis that underwrote and infused American splatter films during the 1960s, 70s and 80s also ushered in a massive transformation of the economy as a whole, when capital propelled itself enthusiastically from manufacture into finance, doing so in such a way as to displace the moving contradiction, but only temporarily. The transformation was from an economy in which value derives solely from productive labour to an economy whose ruling class sought profit through credit and circulation, where there is no value. Here it will be useful to return briefly to some of those theorists with whom we have already spoken.

Giovanni Arrighi concludes a chapter on the long twentieth century with this prophecy: "the newly found prosperity," here born of a transition from production to finance, "rested on a shift of the crisis from one set of relations to another set of relations. It was," he insists, "only a question of time before the crisis would re-emerge in more troublesome forms."[101] In the first decade of the twenty-first century, that remodelled economy met with another major crisis, which is popularly dated to the financial downturn of 2008, or to the upward swing in mortgage-defaults in 2006-07, or to the .com bust of 2000. But, as Joshua Clover reminds us, this crisis really kicked off in the 1970s, on the historical terrain where we encountered the first wave of splatter. "We might say," he writes,

> that the crisis began, in the fullest sense, with the 1973 recession, the oil shocks, the initial collapse of the Bretton Woods agreements, the meteoric ascent of the finance sector, driven by new

markets in derivative assets and by the need to replace fading industrial profits.[102]

If, as Clover avers, we are now encountering a situation in which the "signal and terminal crises bracket a single prolonged event," the question of splatter's economic intelligence, its sensitivity to the moving contradiction, can now be pitted against a second crisis, this time a rupture in the matrix of circulation, whose effect is nevertheless felt just as keenly in the zones of production.

Given all that we now know about the economic intelligence of gore films, perhaps it is unsurprising that this terminal crisis coincides with a second wave of American splatter. With this final chapter I want to emphasize what makes the second wave different from the first, and how some of these differences correspond to the dissimilarity between signal and terminal crises. The argument here is that splatter in these films is an expression of what might be called "the spectacle," and that their narratives actively differentiate between the images of violence and the actuality of pain and suffering. Recall Guy Debord's celebrated clarification: "The spectacle is not a collection of images, but a social relation among people, mediated by images."[103] Gore in these films is part of an illusorily dematerialized image-commodity, but a commodity whose circulation is nonetheless sustained by and simultaneously mediates the old, class-stratified relations of production.

Here we will see how increasingly spectacular scenes of gore and their narrative articulation correspond to the structures of seemingly post-industrial finance. Attending this transformation away from the first wave of splatter, whose films were all about productive labour and its negation, and away from the militant satire of neoliberalism developed in body horror, is another shift in tone. These films are noticeably darker than anything we have looked at so far. Unlike the films we have already seen, whose exuberance derives from their proto-Leninist logic of class warfare or from their satire of ruling-class decadence, these more recent additions to splatter are fogged by an air of desperation – by a typically unsuccessful desire to exit this new social relation, and by an overwhelming sense of nihilism. While it has been argued that these films have something to say about the fluidity of class positions in times of crisis, my intuition is that the shift in tone from revolutionary exuberance to spiteful satire and finally to blighted nihilism speaks to a disillusion of practical leftist politics in the face of crisis. "In order to grasp today's capitalism we need financial analysis," noted Robin Blackburn in 2008, "but the phenomenon of financialization sucks oxygen from the atmosphere."[104] These films realize that the horrors of capital might just be inescapable; and, here, inescapability finds narrative resonance in films whose plots and whose spaces are fatally suffocating.

Post-Socialist Murder Factories

Zingales got at least one thing right. The film that announced American cinema's renewed interest in splatter was indeed *Hostel*. Released commercially in January 2006, this was not the first splatter film of its decade and neither was it the first directed by Roth, who gave us an infectiously grotesque body horror with *Cabin Fever* in 2002, and who more recently paid homage to the Italian cannibal films of the 1970s with *Green Inferno* in 2013. *Hostel* and its 2007 sequel are both set in Slovakia, where a transnational corporation, Elite Hunting, uses a youth hostel to kidnap middle-class tourists, which even wealthier men and woman from multiple nations then pay to murder. The kidnapped tourists are all taken from the hostel to an abandoned factory where they are tortured to death with the generically ubiquitous tools of the trade: chainsaws, blowtorches, scythes, and so on.

In the first film, of the two abducted college students, Josh and Paxton, only the latter escapes, carving his own bloody trail out of Slovakia and into Austria. The sequel, which opens with the escaped Paxton's beheading, engineers a twist on that tale, whose inversion speaks to the director's sensitivity both to issues of gender and sexuality in splatter and to the cognizance of class dynamics during an economic crisis. Rather than following just the victims, this sequel film is equally interested in the murderers, Todd and Stuart, who have paid for the privilege of slaughtering two American college students, Beth and Whitney. However, Beth survives the ordeal, but this is only because she is a multimillionaire heiress who purchases the castration and murder of Stuart and with it her own freedom. She is a final girl, to be sure, but her finality is the result of economic privilege. Between these two films are some important changes in narrative and visual perspective, most notably from the victims in Part I to the aggressors in Part II, but those perspectives are never quite stable. Between them articulates a narrative that grasps the relations of production in the age of finance, glimpsing an economic totality from the ground up.

Beyond the film itself, which we will get to in a moment, *Hostel* was marked as exceptional by the moral panic it galvanized with help from the generic descriptor under which its brand of splatter entered the popular imagination: namely, "torture porn." David Edelstein coined this phrase in a 2006 article that derided the apparent intensification of sadism in mainstream American horror movies:

> Explicit scenes of torture and mutilation were once confined to the old 42nd Street, the Deuce, in gutbucket Italian cannibal pictures like *Make Them Die Slowly*, whereas now they have terrific production values and a place of honor in your local multiplex. As a horror maven who long ago made peace, for better and worse, with the genre's inherent sadism, I'm baffled by how far this new stuff goes – and by why America seems so nuts these days about torture.[105]

While that second noun in "torture porn" is intended as pejorative, a denotation of aesthetic and cultural worthlessness, it also seizes upon the formal continuity between horror and pornography, which we have seen in operation from Lewis' films onward, first as a means of formally cultivating visual pleasure and then in the profusion of weird, nasty, and politically instrumental sex all throughout body horror. Here, however, the fetishism of limbs and organs and the orifice intensifies. It becomes hardcore, so to speak. Though a self-appointed "horror maven," what Edelstein wants from the genre on the whole is morality, whose superimposition helped differentiate the conservative slasher films from the politically radical gore films that preceded them. Or which differentiates Marx from the gothic novelists. In torture porn, we return to the social logic of early splatter, its bleak universalism. Here every character is just as much a victim and an aggressor, similarly to how in the first wave of splatter each body has the potential to dismember. "Some of these movies," claims Edelstein, "are so viciously nihilistic that the only point seems to be to force you to suspend moral judgments altogether."[106] There is no moral compass, only spectacular horror, and yet once again it is precisely because splatter suspends morality that it allows us to think systematically and with clear eyes about the situation it narrates.

Much like the economic climate into which *Hostel* was released, this "new breed of horror" has its origins in an earlier historical moment and an earlier wave of splatter. It is widely known that Roth is a dedicated cinephile, that he is responsible for multiple DVD commentaries on splatter films from the 1970s, including a gloriously bombastic one on *Blood Sucking Freaks*, and that in the two *Hostel* movies he incorporates cameos from older directors in the genre. When Paxton first arrives at the factory, which he has been told is the site for an art exhibition, he crosses paths with a Japanese businessman. The actor here is Takashi Miike, the insanely prolific director of numerous ultraviolent splatter films, including the slow-burn sadism of *Audition*, the familial shockumentary, *Visitor Q*, and the yakuza flick, *Ichi The Killer*. Similarly, the sequel contains a brief glimpse of a minor character's torture, in which he is being eaten alive in a chamber designed for opulence and to a full-blown operatic soundtrack. The cannibal in this scene is played by none other than Ruggero Deodato, the director of *Cannibal Holocaust*. These cameos indicate a heightened awareness of splatter's generic history, but they do so without devolving the film into the kind of self-referential irony that overwhelmed numerous slasher films in the 90s and 2000s. *Hostel* knows exactly where it fits into film history, and like those older, cited films it knows about the economic conditions to which its gore responds.

A return to splatter under the sign of torture has widely been interpreted as a response to American geopolitics, of wars of aggression both imperial and civil, not least because of the similarity between its imagery and the photographs leaked from Abu Ghraib and from Guantanamo Bay in 2003. Roth himself acknowledges this, doing so most explicitly in an interview from 2005: "Thanks to George Bush, Donald Rumsfeld and Dick Cheney we have this whole new wave of horror."[107] And yet, while clearly channelling a discourse of geopolitical terror, which might position such wars outside of the economy, the two *Hostel* films also respond both narratively and aesthetically to their economic situation, thereby suggesting entanglements between aggressor security states, post-socialist ruination, and capitalist accumulation via military dispossession.

Moreover, these films know of their own position at the forefront of a terminal crisis. Both films structure their narratives, as Barry Keith Grant has argued, "in the face of capitalism since, within such a system, we are all commodifiable and consuming bodies,"[108] and here splatter applies within a social relation approximating that of sex slavery. Or, as Aaron Michael Kerner describes the multinational that enables such violence:

> Elite Hunting maintains a strict code of conduct, its underlying principles governed by the application of the most stoic form of free-market capital. Untethered from any sentimentality, the syndicate replicates the will of nature, applying the Darwinian doctrine that only the most (financially) fit survives.[109]

The way these films evolve their shared story of conglomerated torture asks us to generate cognitive maps of an international trade network that extends itself through finance markets and into the heights of economic abstraction, but whose sole source of value remains, as always, labouring and laboured bodies. The films' emphatically post-industrial *mise-en-scène* is important here. The scenes of gore are largely isolated to an abandoned, rust-eaten factory, a forsaken site of manufacture, whose rooms are now used for custom-themed murders. This landscape is one of the privileged sites of postmodern American cinema's historical cartography. "We should love this world," writes Slavoj Žižek about similar terrain in the films of David Lynch, "even its gray decaying buildings and its sulphurous smell – all this stands for history, threatened with erasure between the posthistorical First World and the prehistorical Third World."[110] That interstitial space, between two experientially asymptotic worlds, is shown exactly as an interstice in one remarkable shot that repeats in both films.

When Paxton in Part I and then Todd and Stuart in Part II arrive at the factory, their entrance into the building is depicted from a distance as they cross the floor of its enormous antechamber. This room, shot using a wide-angle lens and with a deep focus, would have once housed massive industrial machinery, but is now hollowed out and empty save for rubble. Shafts of natural light descend through gaping holes in the walls and roof, as though to emphasize that we are neither interior nor exterior. These shots are mournfully beautiful, like something out of an Andrei Tarkovsky picture, but they are also economically intelligent.

What we are seeing here is a passage for the beneficiaries of finance into the apparently obsolete zones of production where, like in the American splatter films made during the signal crisis, unemployed workers turn their trade to new enterprises: this time, their newfound labour is transforming tourists into killable objects, an essential part in the commodity of torture. Indeed, this repeated shot of the antechamber enacts a version of the famous narrative sally performed by Marx in his critique of capitalism. After approximately 150 pages describing the function of monetization and exchange, of finance, and only after having proved categorically that there is no surplus value and therefore no accumulation to be had in the exchange of equivalents, we are asked to finally enter the sphere of manufacture. To learn the source of value. Capitalism's secret. The big reveal:

> Let us therefore, in company with the owner of money and the owner of labour-power, leave this noisy sphere, where everything takes place on the surface and in full view of everyone, and follow them into the hidden abode of production, on whose threshold there hangs the notice 'No admittance except on business'. Here

> we shall see, not only how capital produces, but how capital is itself
> produced. The secret of profit-making must at last be laid bare.[111]

While the antechamber shot repeats in both films, it does so with a significant change of perspective, which is linked to the films as a whole. Part I only shows splatter from the perspective of its victims, from the standpoint of the objects of torture, whereas Part II follows the experience of the torturers. The principal subjectivity in either shot, which in both cases is American, shifts from hazardous naiveté to a position of knowledge. At this point in the narrative, Part I is still exploiting American fears of an Eastern European other, of an alien identity whose experience in the final decades of state socialism render it capable of unthinkable brutality, but Part II is different, manifesting a fraught nostalgia for that second-world coordinate of absolute negation.

If, in Part I, the threat of violence emanates from second-world men and women perceived as culturally primitive by their Anglo-American victims, Part II reveals that the operators of the slaughterhouse are only low-level workers in a much larger company run by a wealthy, cultured capitalist. These Slovakian men and women are the company's real source of value precisely because they undertake the labour of kidnapping and oversee the daily operations in its factory (if the commodity here is the experience of murder, the victims function as a kind of fixed capital, that cannot generate profit but only depreciate, losing value through deformation and becoming worthless upon death). It is thus that Part II carves a bloody passage between two otherwise asymptotic social strata, reconnecting an economy arranged for credit and finance with the wellspring of value, in living labour power.

The scene with which this chapter began emphasized the murderer's role in business – in finance, where "you make money you spend money" – and Part II makes the role of finance important to the murder business around which the two films revolve. In an early scene, we are shown the means by which victims are purchased, using a globally expansive montage that begins when a hostel clerk – familiar from Part I – scans the girls' passport photos into an online auction. This is our introduction to Todd, who makes the purchase on Stuart's behalf while teeing off on a golf course when his phone announces the auction. The scene then cuts to similar scenarios from elsewhere across the world, featuring an obese man lathering a young woman with sunscreen on what appears to be a Mediterranean beach; a Japanese businessman in a glass office flanked by samurai armour; a man in an expensive study, surrounded by ornamental maps and globes; a man outside a French government building; another man on a yacht with his wife; several men with children; one man in a board meeting; and, conspicuous in her gendered singularity, a woman horse-riding. As the bidding war accelerates, the cutting between these shots hastens to match pace, building to a point at which the shot splits into two and then four panels, all featuring close-ups on Beth's image as it appears on smartphones with an escalating price. That all of these figures are the beneficiaries of finance seems bound up in the fact that all of them are wealthy enough to spend hundreds of thousands of dollars on a whim whilst nevertheless being completely decoupled from places of work. With the exception of one participant occupied at the head of a board meeting, all of these men and the one woman are more or less entirely at leisure. They embody the axiomatic notion of finance as "profiting without producing."

And it is the financial market that defines Stuart and ultimately seals his brutal demise. On first encounters, Stuart is portrayed as a middle-class family man, seeing his children off for school, and thoroughly dominated by his wealthier friend, Todd, whom we learn bankrolls their frequent sex tourism. When introduced to his victim, Beth, he is reluctant to murder her. It is only when Todd backs out of murdering Whitney, after tearing off a chunk of her scalp with a circular saw, that Stuart really embraces his designated role of torturer. Todd's attempted abstention is taken as a breach of contract, he is expeditiously torn apart by attack dogs, and a photograph of the patched-up, bleeding-out Whitney is shown to the other torturers. A bargain, but only available for twenty minutes. Stuart takes up the offer, before turning his attentions back to Beth. "Notice something different about me," he scowls upon returning. Face painted in Whitney's blood. "I bet you fucken' do, fucken' bitch. You'll fucken' respect me now." The vocabulary of degrading porn. "I don't fucken' work for you..." Maybe not, but after a quick exchange the men and women of Elite Hunting will find themselves in Beth's employment.

Beth seduces Stuart and easily overpowers him. First with a head-butt, and then with several debilitating blows from a tire iron. "Get in the chair! Get in the fucking chair!" When Beth has chained Stuart to the chair in which he was torturing her, she engineers an escape. She shatters the security camera and demands the door's release code from Stuart. He refuses. She stabs a long, metal hypodermic syringe into his right eardrum. December 12. Beth's birthday. In come the guards. The first is dropped from behind with a blow to the skull, and by the time reinforcements arrive Beth has a handgun trained on them and Stuart taken hostage, with his flaccid genitalia pincered between a pair of shears. She demands to negotiate for her release. "I want to buy my way out of here," she insists, but is told she cannot afford Stuart's murder and her own freedom. "Don't tell me what I can afford," she replies. "There's nothing I can't afford. I could buy and sell everyone in this room." The fury of the financial elite. "Just get me a PDA, a SWIFT number, and a recipient name. I have accounts in Switzerland, Luxemburg, and the Isle of Man. Just name your fucking price!"

When Stuart shouts his complaint – "this is bullshit!" – he is swiftly corrected: "This is business." He offers to pay more, but that idea is put down. "There is a second mortgage on your house. Your daughter's private school tuition. That's why your friend paid." Beth is reminded that money is not the only issue, that there is a contractual obligation to kill. She squeezes the sheers and, in close-up, Stuart's cock and balls are sliced from his abdomen. Canine barking accompanies one long, drawn-out scream. Beth throws the severed genitalia to the dogs. Stuart spasms. "Let him bleed to death." The guards leave the cell, laughing, and slam the door behind them. Stuart's death results directly from the exacting reality principal of the market, in which the brutalization of bodies is ordered only by the highest bidder.

In linking two kinds of capital, the *Hostel* films announce their position within a chronology of economic crises that collapse the distance between finance and production, contracting primarily on the middle-class subjects caught between those two strata. What has changed since the first wave of splatter is that we are no longer seeing the working classes turn against the privileged, or at least they are not doing so unaided or without exploitation. Neither are we seeing a sustained satire directed at the culture of neoliberalism. Rather, we encounter a whole new social relation, in which the elite financial class has orchestrated a bloody intersection between workers and the bourgeoisie. There are, finally, some obvious contextual resonances with this.

The year between which the first and second *Hostel* films were released was that in which the terminal crisis began to resonate within the national imaginary precisely as an event whose effects would be felt far beyond the apparently autonomous spheres of production and finance. During 2007, the year in which *Hostel Part II* was released, lenders commenced foreclosure proceedings on 1.3 million properties, a 79 percent increase on 2006. "It was only in mid-2007," specifies David Harvey,

> when the foreclosure wave hit the white middle class in hitherto booming and significantly Republican urban and suburban areas in the US south (particularly Florida) and west (California, Arizona, and Nevada), that officialdom started to take note and the mainstream press began to comment.[112]

Historically, we have now arrived at a social situation in which the financial elite are culpable for gutting the national economy and for subjugating both a working and a middle class. Stuart's second mortgage comes into view as more than just a narrative fulcrum; it enables a social relation in which the ultra-wealthy outsource and exploit second-world labour to facilitate the murder of predominately middle-class tourists. This is how a terminal crisis looks from the standpoint of splatter.

Fractal Recombinants: Or, The Financial Jigsaw

If the *Hostel* films announced splatter's return to popular cinema, and with that a sustained interest in economics, its commercial viability was ultimately assured by the *Saw* franchise, whose seven films were released between 2004 and 2010. These films' massively convoluted narrative arc, much of which is presented asynchronously and in revelatory flashback, defies any sort of comprehensive summary. It orbits around the serial killer John Kramer, also known as Jigsaw, and his multiple protégés who trap their victims in what he calls "games." These games, which precious few survive, comprise elaborate industrial machinery designed to ironically literalize fatal flaws and to simultaneously test survival instinct through torture.

The games also miniaturize the world of which they are a part. Like the hedge maze in *The Shining*, that spectral afterimage projected from the Overlook's monumental embodiment of an American past, they formalize the passage of capital through financialization. If the Overlook maze is an anachronistic emblem of the superannuated leisure class, the haunting presence of the 1920s into a Cold War setting, the *Saw* traps are a cipher for the 1970s and its crisis in manufacture, as that crisis has come to haunt the first decade of the twenty-first century. The way these films' hyperactive camera navigates through each trap – zooming in and out, accelerating and decelerating, halting here and there – finds its narrative equivalent in the revelatory and totalizing montage sequences that conclude each of the individual films; between the traps and the sequences the films seek to encapsulate the impossibly convoluted structures of finance capital. But before we get to this formal allegory, which would locate history in the *mise-en-scène* and the camerawork, it must be said that these films simultaneously stage their historical moment as narrative content.

That is what we see, for instance, in a moment when one of these games frames itself as a direct response to the financial crisis. The sixth – and most decidedly anti-capitalist – entry in the franchise opens to show a black woman waking up in a room walled by old machinery. Her cranium is engulfed by a spring-loaded metal apparatus, a machine similar to the now iconic reverse bear-trap that recurs elsewhere throughout the franchise. Directly in front of her and on the other side of a metal grate is an overweight white man who remains unconscious. Behind her, on a wooden table, are a rubber tourniquet, a meat cleaver, and a butcher's knife. When she stands, panicking, a lightbulb switches on. The camera arcs 360 degrees around the man, who is now waking up. Mutual recognition. "Eddie," she screams. "Eddie, wake up!" He leans forward, activating another lightbulb as well as an old television set. Its image: a ventriloquist's dummy with a grimy white face, black hair, black-and-red eyes, and red spirals on its cheeks. Its mouth moves in the delivery of a message. This puppet is an avatar for both Kramer and his followers. "Hello," it begins with a line the franchise has elevated to the status of catchphrase. "I want to play a game." The rules are explained forthwith: "The devices on your heads are symbolic of the shackles you place on others. You recklessly loan people money knowing their financial limitations, counting on reposing more than they could ever pay back. You are predators. But today, you become the prey." The puppet draws attention to a scale, their "only path to freedom," into which they are to feed their own "pound of flesh." When a timer reaches one minute, "the one who has given the most flesh will release their bindings while the gears on your opponent's head will engage, piercing their skull."

The game begins in earnest when those gears tighten, screwing steel bolts into both temples, drawing blood, previewing what will happen to one of the two before our eyes in exactly sixty seconds time. "I'm not dying for you, bitch," shouts the man while lifting up his shirt to expose rolls of fat, into which he begins carving with the butcher's knife. She, the much slimmer of the pair, mimics the gesture in what is surely a moment of comedy – looking down at taut abs as though discovering for the first time that she has no fat to cut away – before applying the tourniquet to her left arm. The camera cuts back and forth between them at breakneck pace. He slices off a chunk of his stomach and drops it onto the scale. The clock is ticking. She moves her own knife further and further up her arm – from the fingers, to the forearm–

and begins sawing. He carves off another chunk, exposing a cavernous wound. Shades of Monsieur Creosote. Her efforts to hack off the limb are stymied by bone. She moves further up the arm, to the joint, and makes another incision. Time is running out. The intercutting accelerates. Twenty seconds remain. The woman takes up the cleaver and hews off her own arm – only it takes multiple blows to hammer through the bone, all the while her adversary continues pulling out pieces of his torso and dropping them into the scale. The arm finally comes clean and though in serious shock she stumbles to the scale and drops in the severed limb, which outweighs the opposing heap of fat, and the clock reaches one minute. We have a winner. Bolts drill into the fat man's temples, killing him, and the scene fades out over the woman's distorted screaming.

While scenarios like this are explicable enough and invariably make for spectacularly gory deaths – or, sometimes, for equally gory escapes – what would render a detailed plot summary of the franchise significantly more bewildering are the multiple asynchronous layers of narrative and the vast web of characters forever dropping in and out of action. Invoking something of Alfred Hitchcock, this series appeals to the paranoid convolutions of the old conspiracy thrillers. Over its seven-film arc seemingly minor characters and victims presumed dead return unexpectedly. Major characters have double and sometimes triple motives. While the films' source of gore is consistently in the games, Kramer, a living embodiment of the Jigsaw moniker, dies of cancer in the third film. And yet, after his death, the legacy is pursued by several protégés, all of whom are trained to emulate their master. In this way, the ventriloquist's dummy we encountered on screen becomes a disembodied symbol for the violence, a floating image behind which any person can occupy the Jigsaw subject position. Here, as in the second-world factories of *Hostel*, we encounter an economy that ostensibly decouples the machinery of splatter, the games themselves, from the multimedia spectacle of their execution. Indeed, the gore is always mediated and remediated through a vast web of analogue tapes and circuits and through various digital signals, all of which distort narrative temporality, swapping out cause and effect, blending it all into an unstable totality.

In this case, splatter takes place under the sign of what Franco Berardi calls "semio-capital," which he describes as "a form of social production which is essentially focused on the production of signs," and which he periodises as "the sphere of the increasing replacement of production by a financial - and financial means de-territorialised - and fractal-recombinant form of production."[113] Note the Deleuzian term, de-territorialised, a neoliberal watchword that should echo the philosophy used to introduce the social logic satirized in our previous chapter. In this instance, however, I want to underscore and expand upon the neologism, "fractal-recombinant," because it will help us grasp these particular films' formal and narrative convolutions. In Berardi's account, "if you look at the financial game you see that the real world is simultaneously broken up into infinite fragments and continuously recombined into a new form, a new gestalt, or figure."[114] Material and social phenomena are "fractalized" when the old structures of capital break down, because of the moving contradiction, and they are "recombined" by the force of credit and finance, which have come to exert hegemony over the economy as a whole. Mediated by the spectacle are the relations of production, which have been broken down and atomized by neoliberal ideology but reassembled along the intractable lines of class division – just like a jigsaw. And indeed, the vast and conspiratorial plot of the *Saw* films occupies that de-territorialized world of an outwardly post-industrial economy, a void beneath the credit market into which the old relations of production reassemble themselves, horrifically.

A principle aesthetic continuity between *Hostel* and *Saw* is their post-industrial *mise-en-scène*. While Roth's films were set in post-Soviet Europe, in the *Saw* franchise we inhabit American cities with the look and feel of any given East Coast ruin, but whose superabundance of unoccupied factory space suggests that we are in one of the smaller post-industrial zones, such as Detroit, Pittsburgh, or Buffalo. Despite the North American setting, we are presented once again with a decidedly second-world means of production and a city from which productive labour has been outsourced, offshored, and blighted with austerity. We enter the horror of urban wreckage. What this leaves, however, are the spaces and the machines of manufacture which are, in these films, brought to life once more and in elaborate reconfigurations so as to inflict themselves on more and differently classed bodies. Jigsaw's traps restage industrial capitalism's uttermost bloody machinations: machines that pierce, twist, scalp, and sever; electrified metal; pits of biomedical waste; scorching steam; poisonous gas; freezing water; face-melting acid; and so on. Here the frequently middle-class victims are forced into the position of industrial workers and are destroyed by heavy machinery in such ways as to simulate occupational injuries. Small wonder those victims are pushed toward regularly fatal self-harm by way of omnipresent clocks and timers, capitalism's chief measurement device for the extraction of value.

These games are most grotesque when most obviously recreating the scenarios of industrial manufacture – and the most stomach-churning of all returns us yet again to that primal figure of all splatter: the *Gallerte*. The third film's game focuses on Jeff, a man who succumbed to alcoholism after the death of his son at the hands of a drunk driver. He is tested at an abandoned meatpacking plant in which he is required to save those responsible for his son's death and for the killer's acquittal. The judge that presided over the case, and who acquitted the killer, is strapped down to the bottom of an empty vat. Several rotten, maggot-riddled pig carcasses are hoisted overhead and dropped into an industrial meat grinder, so that the liquefied remains are spewed out onto the judge. Jeff is forced to burn his son's possessions to locate a key for the judge's bindings. Before the judge is extracted he becomes fully submerged in the grey-brown slurry and awash in bloated entrails. This scene is totally disgusting. You can just about smell the rancid stench of death and decay. Here, as elsewhere throughout the franchise, a reasonably wealthy subject is forced to occupy the role and suffer the fate of an industrial worker. Under the Jigsaw image, class fractals are recombined to fill a void in the economy. But why should the film so obviously, so consciously restage what is almost a caricature of large-scale industry? It would seem to have the same nostalgia for massive and complex machinery that the earlier splatter films have for power tools.

Only after Kramer's death are his motives and his training revealed. Before commencing his tenure as Jigsaw, Kramer was a successful civil engineer, devoted husband, and soon-to-be father. After his wife miscarried their unborn child due to the careless assault of a drug addict, a woman who slams his wife behind a clinic door, Kramer withdrew from domestic life and was soon diagnosed with inoperable cancer. Kramer was then "reborn" in an almost Christian sense after his failed suicide, from which he distilled the idea of rehabilitation through torture and potential death. There is a weird irony to the primary cause of all this: while Kramer's wife is assaulted whilst working in a clinic for those who can't afford health insurance, Kramer's insurers nevertheless deny him the experimental medical treatment, which he could afford but which he then refuses only on principle. Unlike the men and women at the clinic, Kramer is not a victim of circumstance, or at least not in the same way.

The situation in which Jigsaw is forged is therefore defined by massive reductions to public provisions across a range of fields, including housing, health, education, and pensions, and therefore is one of increasing privatization and, significantly, of an expanded market for insurance. Costas Lapavitsas provides an accurate description of how this manifestly neoliberal situation is essential to the rise of financial hegemony. "Private finance," he says, "has emerged as the mediator of private provision across these fields, even though it has no evident skills in delivering such services and even if its performance has often been predatory and crisis-prone."[115] Kramer's philosophy hinges on a libertarian commitment to personal accountability, a punitive logic of individual will against any and all social adversity. Here Kramer the engineer begins to look like Howard Roark the architect, and with that the Jigsaw murders reveal themselves for what they truly are: the application of neoliberal ideology to a society now gutted by finance. Recall that, in *The Texas Chain Saw Massacre*, the disenfranchised abattoir workers put their skills to work in new settings. That logic works both up and down the class spectrum. Here, similarly, Kramer makes use of his skills precisely as an entrepreneur – as a gifted engineer who was setting up a business at the time of personal loss, and who now employs his engineering skills to create elaborate torture machines and whose business acumen translates into the management of disciples who ably make good on a legacy. Under Kramer, torture has become a franchise. Jigsaw is its brand name.

We Are All Human Centipedes Now!

If, in American cinema, splatter returns from within a terminal crisis as torture porn, whose major iterations help illustrate that this crisis is not just financial but more generally economic, that it too is grounded in material production, the return has not been geographically singular. Elsewhere across the globe, torture porn has keyed itself into national myths and localized manifestations of the moving contradiction. In Eastern Europe, in the formerly socialist countries now faced with shock doctrine, capitalist subsumption is portrayed as a bloody, carnal assault on the body. That assault is staged with merciless clarity in *Taxidermia* (2006) and *A Serbian Film* (2010). In Western Europe, and especially in France, class conflict, political polarization, and the emergence of neo-fascism have given rise to a spray of vicious films, the most socially engaged of which include *Frontier(s)* (2007), *Inside* (2007), and *Martyrs* (2008). East Asia, though better known to Anglophone audiences for its high-tech ghost stories, has delivered multiple ultra-violent flicks. These range from the camp lunacy of *Tokyo Gore Police* (2008) to the truly disquieting *Grotesque* (2009). Then there is the legion of films within which the agrestic lumpen seek retribution, perhaps most effectively in *Eden Lake* (2008) from the United Kingdom and in the two *Wolf Creek* films from Australia (2005, 2013). From within this fully globalized context, in which cinematic gore marries itself to the local permutations of economic strife, the allegorical impulses that find expression in the *Hostel* and *Saw* films reach their conceptual acme with a now infamous trilogy that begins in Germany, passes through England, to finally arrive in America. The trilogy is, of course, *The Human*

Centipede, devised and directed by conceptual mastermind Tom Six. Its three films comprise the titular insect's three bodily segments, an imbricated form that snakes its way around the globe: *First Sequence* (2009), *Full Sequence* (2011), and *Final Sequence* (2015).

The ordurous concept behind these films is, in a sense, more memorable than the films themselves – and this in itself is important, but more on that later. The concept entails surgically conjoining a group of mutilated humans, mouth to ass and ass to mouth, and thereby creating an interorganic arthropod with a single, shared digestive tract. Here is the "medically accurate" description given by the first film's surgeon, Dr Josef Heiter, to his three kidnapped patients, A, B, and C, as accompanied by their tortured screams and his jarringly cartoonish diagrams:

> We start with cutting the ligamentum patellae, the ligaments of the kneecaps, so knee extension is no longer possible. Pull from B and C the central incisors, the lateral incisors and canines from the upper and lower jaws. The lips from B and C, and the anus of A and B are cut circular along the border between skin and mucosa, the mucous cutaneous zone. Two pedicled grafts are prepared and lifted from their underlying tissue. The V-shaped incisions below the chins of B and C up to the cheeks, connecting the circular mucosa and skin parts of anus and mouth from A to B and B to C. Connect the pedicled grafts to the chin-cheek incisions from A to B and B to C, creating a Siamese triplet, connected via the gastric system. Ingestion by A passes through B to the excretion of C. *A human centipede, first sequence.*

While this description might be clinical, its actualization is much less so. The relatively fortunate individual at the front or head of the centipede can eat normally enough, but the person behind them and grafted facially to their asshole is forced into a diet of human excrement and nothing else, which is then re-digested and passed along back to the third person, the only part capable of normal excretion. Here torture marries itself to coprophilia. Infections abound.

The three films construct human centipedes of varying lengths and under vastly different conditions of production.

In *First Sequence*–whose plot-points echo *Hostel*–a German doctor with a specialty in separating conjoined twins abducts three tourists: two female, from America, and one male, from Japan, which are then stitched together into a triple-bodied monstrosity and forced to shuffle around its creator's ultra-modern compound. Things get weirder and nastier with the *Full Sequence*, which relocates from Germany to England, where an overweight, poor, and mentally-disturbed man has become obsessed with the first film. He kidnaps twelve individuals–including the actress, Ashlynn Yennie, caught in the middle of the first centipede–and, under extraordinarily less hygienic conditions and with zero surgical expertise, he joins them together with masking tape and a staple gun. Whereas the first film kept a lot of the operation off-screen and relatively sanitary, this much grimier sequel relishes the blood and the excrement, which together seem to spray across every surface and with the same inky blackness. It takes the concept of the first film and recasts it within one man's exceedingly twisted psychosexual fantasy. *Final Sequence* returns both actors from the first two films, the German scientist played by Dieter Laser and the English lunatic played by Laurence R. Harvey, who now ham it up as a prison warden and his bumbling accountant. Accents and affectations are modified accordingly. While the scientist becomes a German-American, our London lunatic goes all out and embraces the role of Southern gentleman. This film, set somewhere in the American Southwest, also has its characters take inspiration from the first two films, which leads to their cost-efficient solution for overpopulated and underfunded prisons: a vast, five-hundred-person centipede, which requires no security personnel and very little in the way of sustenance.

The overall aesthetic changes severely from one sequence to the next, perhaps most obviously in the use of colour, from the mutely desaturated palette of the first, through the black-and-white high-contrasts of the second, to the garish vibrancy of the third. That change not only responds to shifts in cultural context but also evolves the tone from that of a relatively conventional torture porn film, through to something reaching for the technical achievements of Bergman-esque art cinema, to finally resemble a classic-era splatter film, redolent of Herschell Gordon Lewis in its overblown colouration as well as in its irrepressible schlockiness. Indeed, as one unfairly condescending review describes the third instalment:

> This is the first new film I've seen in a while that made me feel like it was made in the same vein as *Blood Feast*, an incompetent 1963 horror film that took films from the intentionally off-putting Grand Guignol theater, and sold itself to drive-in and grindhouse attendants as 'the first splatter film.'[116]

And yet, despite the massive differences between these three films, they all share a debt to at least one filmic antecedent.

"For me," Six tells us, "the most influential and original film is *Salò* by Pasolini," a film to which he attributes "an everlasting impression."[117] That impression carries through as direct influence into the human centipede trilogy, which conspicuously replicates several of its shots, not to mention the repetition of that earlier film's reviling coprophilia. These shots include the parading of young, naked captives on hands and knees and in bondage; the forceful extraction of a tongue; and the witnessing of mass torture from a distance and through binoculars – all of which not only restage Pasolini's *mise-en-scène* but also adapt his framing. Moreover, what these films also seem to inherit from Pasolini is that director's aesthetic ideology – his instrumental deployment of gore to amplify a disgust with biopolitical despotism if not actual fascism. Dr Heiter, whose first name really is Josef, imports shades of the Holocaust into the German ruling class from Angela Merkel's era of rule. Martin's plight responds to a sexually abusive state apparatus and to a homicidally incestuous family. And finally, the prison in which the third film is set ham-handedly reprimands the American government for the War on Terror. We are in the "George H. W. Bush Prison," the inmates all wear iconic, orange jumpsuits, are subject to sadistically enhanced versions of water-boarding, and their torture is announced by the unhinged prison warden as a bid to go "Guantanamo style." There are some obvious parallels with Roth in this. "I'm being satirical," Six has claimed of his solution to prison overcrowding, "but I think the Bush administration might be interested."[118]

Anti-fascism, certainly, but there is an equally if not more compelling argument to be made that these films are just as much about capitalism, delivering up a resplendently literal rendition of trickle-down economics for the age of liberal pluralism. Reza Negarestani develops a version of such an argument with bracing acuity in an unpublished essay, the abstract for which bears quotation:

> But this is a world in which the financial closure of capitalism is cloned and grafted onto a cognitively maimed economy for accumulating false alternatives in the name of liberation of imagination and action. A suture of different overambitious vocations and driven by the wealth of waste it generates, the resulting beast is a prophetic vision of a tightly connected and controlled society with a single closed alimentary circuit, the human centipede. Those who scheme to infiltrate this world in order to militantly or cunningly liberate it from the inside are locked into the compactly segmented structure of the metameric organism.[119]

Despite the divergence in geopolitical and cultural context between Germany, England, and the United States, the centipedes all manifest their own special breed of inclusiveness. Quoting the prison warden: "A Jew behind a Muslim, a Muslim behind a Jew, a Republican behind a Mexican, a Crip behind a Blood, peace on earth and goodwill to men." In this sense, there is an approximation of equality to be had with or even within the human centipede, in that no matter his or her race or creed everyone is entitled to the same shit-eating fate. This universalization of torture, its omnipresent brutality, has not gone unnoticed. When explaining why the BBFC refused to classify the second sequence, the statement given was that this film is unclassifiable because, in its commitment to "the spectacle of the total degradation," it forges a strong link between sexual arousal and extreme violence. "There is little attempt to portray any of the victims in the film as anything other than objects to be brutalised and degraded for the amusement and sexual arousal of the main character and for the pleasure of the viewer."[120]

A situation in which all personal value is indexed to one's capacity for objectification is, of course, that founding premise of capitalism, a social organism which "is by nature a leveller, since it exacts in every sphere of production equality in the conditions of the exploitation of labor..."[121] Indeed, capitalism produces a uniquely debased collectivism in which, as with Negarestani's description of the human centipede, everyone is both "necessary for the growth yet expendable, every insider is a new addition to the iterated sequence of mouths and rectums," or, as another reviewer puts it in a brilliant phrase that perfectly captures the experience of life in labour, these films orchestrate "the most depressing conga line you've ever seen in your life."[122] Solidarity is bisected into unrecognizable yet absolutely interdependent parts, with digestion serving as socially necessary labour time, all of which produces a social being for which the only available collective is not liberating but utterly horrifying.

But where does this leave finance, that manifestation of capitalism into whose crisis these films were released? Like the *Saw* films, in which Jigsaw's complex traps are emblematic of the saga's totalizing plot and of that plot's recasting of its economic context, this trilogy also cultivates the correlation between its narrative and the means by which it depicts gore. The films themselves, as a trilogy, combine into their own meta-textual centipede. The first sequence inaugurates the concept, and exists as a stand-alone, self-contained narrative; the second film begins with its antagonist watching the first film's ending, from which he is inspired to create a human centipede of his own; and the third begins with its antagonists, played by the same actors from the first two films, as they are watching the second film's ending, which shows that film's antagonist watching the first film's ending, and from which they too are inspired to create a human centipede.

The law of diminishing returns that applies so unremittingly to the nutritional value of digestive matter within the human centipede simultaneously exerts itself upon the films' concept, whose shock value lessens with every reiteration. While there are clear allegorical resonances between this and the moving contradiction's falling rate of profit—which finds its ultimate destination in an overpopulation of living labour power, and so in overcrowded prisons – I want to conclude the chapter here by suggesting that it is precisely this feature, the way the trilogy handles its own diminishing shock value over three intercalated iterations, that speaks directly to the structure of finance, on two distinct levels. This is going to get a little complicated.

Attentive readers might have noticed something eccentric about this part of our discussion – that this is the first splatter film we have looked at to which I haven't spent at least a few sentences describing any particular scene or sequence. There is good reason for this. Some might suggest that more affecting than visuals of the human centipede, more so than its procedural generation and its bodily functions, is the immaterial and potentially immortal idea: what Hegel would call the Notion or *Begriff* of a shared digestive system. Indeed, once you think it you can't unthink it. Perhaps more than any other horror film, this trilogy seems to live and die in its concept – the title alone, with its awesome power of suggestion, potentially eclipses the gore of the visuals. Simply drop it into conversation and you'll see what I mean. In that sense, we are once again dealing with the spectacle, a film whose analogy to finance and to financial abstraction derives from the fact that its selling point is an image that mediates social relations – or, in this case, an idea or concept that governs the manipulation of filmic materials. But this relationship, between the idea and the thing itself, works both ways.

The trilogy's evolving taglines give the game away here. First "100% Medically Accurate," then "100% Medically Inaccurate," and finally "100% Politically Incorrect." The irony is that, as the films claim to move further and further beyond the reality principal and into the realm of pure political ideation, they simultaneously proceed, narratively, toward some final revelation of the underlying real, that elusive social object beyond the idea. In consuming the first two films – whose DVDs are screened as instructive material for the centipede-destined prisoners; and whose director, Tom Six, appears as a consultant, the character "Tom Six" – the third sequence simultaneously acknowledges the purely fictional status of the original human centipede, as well as the fact that another film has already taken inspiration from that human centipede to imagine its own monstrosity. Yet this third and "final" film nevertheless commits to its own even more elaborate production which, by virtue of its inhabiting a reality that contains the previous two films, is more real. While, on the surface, these films present a leap from medically accurate manufacture to the politically incorrect circulation of a medically inaccurate idea, they also know that their shock value is unsustainable via the circulation of that idea alone. Instead, the idea requires material production, and the production of longer and longer centipedes comprising more and more exploited humans, until we arrive at a point when, by the third film's conclusion, what was initially shocking is now just absurd, but, from the standpoint of quantity, it is so much worse. This chiasmus in which quality and quantity mutate into one another posits a sense of the reality within the illusion. It suggests the irreducible materiality of what Marx calls fictitious capital. The trilogy, as a whole, follows the path of financialization as an abstraction from the real, but that abstraction leads right back to crisis, when the law of value reasserts itself via an inability to sustain the shocking force of that initial idea.

This is the structure of our own terminal crisis, of a historical moment when the absence of real value has finally asserted itself over paper profits. But the moment is no longer exclusively American. The chiasmus of production and finance plays out not just between ideas and material, between the market and manufacture, but also across zones of geopolitical sovereignty, each with their own internal systems of accumulation. That these films stage the intestinal conjunction of Germany, England, and the United States – conjoining them into a singular monolithic entity – speaks to the view of capitalism as an integrated system of systems, to the fact that multiple states must be interconnected to promote the hegemony of one, which in the present economic cycle remains American. If each body is its own sovereign zone of production, the combination of multiple bodies is the task of the market. It is thus that finance transgresses the political sovereignty of these otherwise independent zones, so that the market effectively constructs a shared digestive system between capitalist superpowers. Germany, England, and the United States are three of the four major countries committed to finance – the other shares its nationality with that man at the front of the original human centipede – and it is the abstracted idea, notion, or concept, the imagined possibility of a human centipede, which in these films holds them together, guaranteeing the flow of excremental matter from one state to the others, and from the others to one. It's the most horrible and horrifying story you can ever imagine. We're all in it, stitched together. Ass to mouth. Its name is capitalism, and it's choking to death on its own shit.

Coda

Change Mummified

First the music. Our soundtrack is "Free Bird," by Lynyrd Skynyrd, an old road song whose long and desolate overture will eventually explode into a hot frenzy of wailing guitars. Now the visuals. Filmed from above and in a wide-angle shot, we look down on three figures packed into a top-down muscle car as it winds a route along the desert highways. Otis, Spaulding, and Baby. Barely alive. This is what remains of the Firefly family, a clan of homicidally anti-federalist lumpens. All three are covered in gore and ash from the night's ordeal, when they faced off against the full might of a police vendetta. Otis drives. Spaulding and Baby sleep in the backseat. The scene cuts between Otis' weary, road-locked gaze and halcyon video footage of all three travellers together, living happily in much better times. Nostalgia and melancholy intermix as fantasy. The car pulls to a halt and the camera cranes up and overhead. A close-up on Otis as he grips the wheel, then, in the reverse-shot: a police blockade, stretching from one side of the highway to the other, completely unassailable. His head drops backward onto the restraint. Grim resignation. End of the line.

He wakes the two passengers. Both cry out injured and spit blood before recognizing what's before them. Otis hands back the guns: for Baby, a six-shot revolver; for Spaulding, a pump-action shotgun. Locked, loaded, and staring down a shit-scared police force, Baby shouts in silence. We don't hear the words but can read her lips. Two words, perfectly articulated: "Mother. Fucker." Their car accelerates and so does the song. Guitars wail. Shots fire both ways. All three take hits. Spaulding is thrown back. Then Baby. The sequence begins to blur, the reel stalling and stretching. A bullet hole in Baby's right arm. And then her shoulder rips open. The soundtrack distorts. Silence. The film grinds to a halt, as though caught on the spool and ready to burn. A frozen image of Baby. Then it all starts up again but without sound. Something is broken. The film itself, the apparatus that sustains these images, is malfunctioning. Otis screams. Then Spaulding. Silence. Asynchronous gunfire. Fade to black. Roll the credits.

"Change mummified." This is what André Bazin might have called the effect in which a photographic image stills the flow of filmic animation.[123] The scene concludes Rob Zombie's sophomore triumph, *The Devil's Rejects*, which was released in 2005 at the onset of the terminal crisis and the beginning of American splatter's second wave of popularity. With its unresolved ending and its stuttering mechanism, a formal redoubling of its narrative termination, this film delivers an almost perfect figure for where we have arrived historically.

The majority of this book was written in the final months of 2015. The present cycle of accumulation has come to an end. American hegemony is collapsing in the force of a terminal crisis. Capitalism has driven headlong into an unassailable blockade of the moving contradiction, and though it wants to evolve, to relocate its regions of production, accumulation, and profit, the viability of perpetual relocation finds itself outvied by another crisis. This crisis is not just American. It is world-historical and absolute. Given capitalism's need to amass profits elsewhere, to constantly rezone its methods of value extraction outward into new frontiers, where will it go from here? Can the mode of production sustain itself when materially circumscribed by the world-system's geographical limits? What next?

It's not just the Firefly clan that hit a blockade. The filmic apparatus, that material substrate of their narrative being, also begins tearing itself apart. Older forms and antiquated media reassert themselves. This too could be allegorical. Without an immediate replacement for the United States, the mode of production is stalled and stuttering. Against this, allegedly outmoded forms of sociality and of politics are stirring with new life. And, for just as long, splatter seems to have been caught by the same circumstances, which have taken the shape of an almost melancholic nostalgia: just try to count how many gore films have been remade, rebooted, and homaged in the fallout of our terminal crisis, as well as how many horror films more generally have been remade precisely as gore films. Perhaps this tendency is most emblematic of all, their nostalgia and their melancholy, given the directionless moment on which they now fall. Capital has not recovered from its terminal crisis, and yet it still persists, refusing both reconstruction and an irrevocable demise. The violence is universal and absolute, but it has not yet peaked. Change: mummified.

Endnotes

1 Randy Palmer, *Herschell Gordon Lewis, Godfather of Gore: The Films*. North Carolina: McFarland and Company. p. 64.

2 Theodor Adorno, *Minima Moralia: Reflections on a Damaged Life*. London & New York: Verso, 1951. p. 226.

3 Siegfried Kracauer, *From Caligari to Hitler: A Psychological History of the German Film*. Princeton: Princeton UP, 1947. pp. 5-6.

4 Colin Milburn, *Nanovision: Engineering the Future*. Durham and London: Duke UP, 2008. p. 168.

5 John McCarty, *Splatter Movies: Breaking the Last Taboo on Screen*. New York: St Martins Press, 1984. Here it should be said that, beyond McCarty's book, there is relatively little scholarship dedicated solely to splatter, which often gets folded into a different type of horror film: the slasher. For a truly indispensable resource, however, see the encyclopedic "Gorehound's Guide" books by Scott Aaron Stine.

6 Fredric Jameson. *Signatures of the Visible*. 1990. London and New York: Routledge, 2007. p. 29.

7 Quoted in Georg Lukács, "Critical Observations on Rosa Luxemburg's 'Critique of the Russian Revolution.'" *History and Class Consciousness*. Trans. Rodney Livingstone. Cambridge: MIT Press, 1971. pp. 277-278.

8 Karl Marx, *Capital: A Critique of Political Economy, Vol. 1, The Process of Capitalist Accumulation*. Trans. Samuel Moore and Edward Aveling. Ed. Friedrich Engels. Chicago: Charles H. Kerr & Company, 1906. p. 470. This is a print version of the PDF that circulates online, and which is hosted at Marxists.org.

9 Marx, *Grundrisse: Foundations of the Critique of Political Economy*. Trans. Martin Nicolaus. London: Penguin, 1993.

10 Marx, *Capital*. p. 181-2.

11 Giovanni Arrighi, *The Long Twentieth Century: Money, Power, and the Origin of Our Times*. 1994. London: Verso, 2010. On all of this I remain hugely

indebted to poet-critic Joshua Clover, whose work has done plenty to secure the place of political economy, and in particular Arrighi's systemic view of history, as a viable avenue for the discussion of aesthetic forms. For a condensed rehearsal of similar conceptual material to which I present here, see Joshua Clover, "Value | Crisis | Theory." *PMLA* 127:1 (January 2012). p. 112.

12   Leo Panitch and Sam Gindin, *The Making of Global Capitalism: The Political Economy of the American Empire*. London & New York: Verso, 2012. p. 135.

13   Arrighi, *The Long Twentieth Century*. p. 356.

14   Steven Shaviro, *Post Cinematic Affect*. Winchester: Zero, 2010. Ebook.

15   John-Paul Sartre, *Search for a Method*. Trans. H. Barnes. New York: Vintage, 1963. p. 44.

16   Scott Weinberg, "Bloodsucking Freaks." Efilmcritic. com. 2000. Web. 1 April 2016.

17   For a detailed account of New York City's economic blight and its neoliberal redevelopment – another blight, really – during this time, see Chapter 3, "Werewolf Hunger," in Alberto Toscano and Jeff Kinkle, *Cartographies of the Absolute* (Alresford: Zero, 2014). Ebook.

18   Jameson, *Signatures*. p. 29.

19   Vladimir Lenin, "The Military Programme of the Proletarian Revolution: II." Marxists.org. 1916. Web. 1 April 2016.

20   Adorno, *Negative Dialectics*. London and New York: Routledge, 1973. p. 122.

21   Jameson, *Postmodernism: Or, The Cultural Logic of Late Capitalism*. London and New York: Verso, 1991. p. 5.

22   Philip Mirowski, *Never Let A Serious Crisis Go to Waste: How Neoliberalism Survived the Financial Meltdown*. London and New York: Verso, 2013. p. 2.

23   Franco Moretti, *Signs Taken for Wonders: On the Sociology of Literary Forms*. London and Verso: 2005. p. 83.

24 Bram Stoker, *Dracula*. Eds. Nina Auerbach and David J. Skal. 1897. New York: Norton, 1997. pp. 53-4.

25 Mary Shelley, *Frankenstein: The Original 1818 Text*. Eds. D. L. Macdonald and Kathleen Scherf. Broadview: Ontario,1999. p. 79.

26 Shelley, *Frankenstein*. p. 82

27 Shelley, *Frankenstein*. p. 85.

28 Stoker, *Dracula*. p. 53.

29 Stoker, *Dracula*. p. 192.

30 Stoker, *Dracula*. p. 324.

31 David McNally, *Monsters of the Market: Zombies, Vampires and Global Capitalism*. Leiden: Brill, 2010. p. 114.

32 Marx, *Capital*. p. 257.

33 Marx, *Capital*. p. 217.

34 Chris Harman, *Zombie Capitalism: Global Crisis and the Relevance of Marx*. Chicago: Haymarket, 2009. p. 80.

35 Marx, *Capital*. p. 834.

36 Marx, *Capital*. pp. 329-30.

37 Marx, *Capital*. p. 626.

38 Marx, *Capital*. p. 561.

39 Keston Sutherland, *Stupefaction: A Radical Anatomy of Phantoms*. London: Seagull, 2011. pp. 37-51.

40 Sutherland, *Stupefaction*. p. 42.

41 David Bordwell, "Monumental Heroics: Form and Style in Eisenstein's Silent Films." *The Silent Cinema Reader*. Eds. Lee Grieveson and Peter Krämer. London and New York: Routledge, 2004. p. 378.

42 Bordwell, "Monumental Heroics." pp. 386-7.

43 Sergei Eisenstein, *Film Form: Essays in Film Theory*. Trans, Jay Leyda. San Diego: Harcourt, 1949. p. 16.

44 Eisenstein, "Notes for a Film of 'Capital.'" Trans. Maciej Sliwowski, Jay Leyda and Annette Michelson. *October* 2 (Summer, 1976). p. 23.

45 Eisenstein, "Montage of Attractions: For 'Enough Stupidity in Every Wiseman.'" Trans. Daniel Gerould. *The Drama Review: TDR*. 18.1. (March 1974). p. 78.

46   Eisenstein, *Selected Works*. Vol. 1. Ed. and Trans.
      Richard Taylor. London: British Film Institute,
      1988. p. 41.

47   Evan Calder Williams, *Combined and Uneven
      Apocalypse: Luciferian Marxism*. Winchester:
      Zero, 2010. p, 209.

48   Stanley Cavell, *Cavell on Film*. New York: State
      University of New York Press, 2005. p. 26.

49   Michael Haneke, Interviewed by Luisa Zielinski. "The
      Art of Screenwriting No. 5." *The Paris Review*
      211 (Winter 2014). Web. 1 April 2016.

50   Karl Marx and Friedrich Engels. *The Marx-Engels
      Reader*. Second Edition. Ed. Robert C. Tucker. New York:
      Norton, 1978. pp. 482-3.

51   How do you judge the impact of scholarly research
      beyond categorically awful metrics? To my
      knowledge, Carol Clover is the only theorist of
      cinematic horror to have had a film made following
      her coinage. Not once, but twice. *The Final Girls* was
      directed by Todd Strauss-Schulson and released in
      2015; and, though it is less of a horror film, 2015 also
      saw the release of *Final Girl*, directed by Tyler Shields.
      There's an argument to be made, too, that Clover
      effectively wrote the playbook for the ultra-popular
      Scream franchise.

52   Carol J. Clover, *Men, Women, and Chain Saws: Gender
      in the Modern Horror Film*. Princeton: Princeton UP,
      2015. pp. 22-3.

53   Clover, *Men, Women, and Chain Saws*. p. 60.

54   Clover, *Men, Women, and Chain Saws*. p. 115.

55   Clover, *Men, Women, and Chain Saws*. p. 163.

56   Kim Newman, *Nightmare Movies: Wide Screen Horror
      Since 1968*. New Jersey: Proteus Books, 1984. p. 9.

57   Laura Mulvey, *Visual and Other Pleasures*. Basingstoke:
      Palgrave Macmillan, 1989. p. 19.

58   Sharviro, "Avant-Prof: An Interview With Steve
      Shaviro" *The Write Stuff*. n. d. Web. 1 April 2016.

59   Kjetil Rødje, *Images of Blood in American Cinema:
      The Tingler to The Wild Bunch*. London and New York:
      Routledge. Ebook.

60 Rødje, *Images of Blood in American Cinema*. Ebook.
61 Robert Brenner, *The Economics of Global Turbulence: The Advanced Capitalist Economies from Long Boom to Long Downturn, 1945–2005*. London and New York: Verso, 2006.
62 Arrighi, *The Long Twentieth Century*. p. 307.
63 Robin Wood, *Hollywood from Vietnam to Reagan... and Beyond*. New York: Columbia UP, 2003. p. 82.
64 Tobe Hooper, Interviewed by Keith Phipps. *The AV Club*. 11 October 2000. Web. 1 April 2016.
65 Clover, *Men, Women, and Chain Saws*. p. 32.
66 Ben A. Hervey, *Night of the Living Dead*. Basingstoke: Palgrave Macmillan, 2008. p. 57.
67 Barry Keith Grant, *The Dread of Difference: Gender and the Horror Film*. Austin: University of Texas Press, 2015. p. 230.
68 Harman, *Zombie Capitalism*. p. 12.
69 Edward P. Comentale and Aaron Jaffe, *The Year's Work at the Zombie Research Center*. Bloomington and Indianapolis: Indiana UP, 2014. p. 14.
70 Marx, *Capital*. p. 217.
71 Harry Braverman, *Labor and Monopoly Capital: The Degradation of Work in the Twentieth*. New York: Monthly Review Press, 1998. p. 22.
72 Michael A. Arnzen, "Who's Laughing Now? The Postmodern Splatter Film." *Journal of Popular Film and Television* 21.4 (1994). p. 178.
73 Glauber Rocha, "The Aesthetics of Hunger." *Film Manifestos and Global Cinema Cultures: A Critical Anthology*. Ed. Scott MacKenzie. Berkeley: University of California press, 2014. p. 219.
74 Ernest Mandel, *Late Capitalism*. London: Humanities Press, 1975. p. 23.
75 Glauber Rocha, "The Aesthetics of Hunger." p. 219.
76 Gilles Deleuze and Félix Guattari, *Anti-Oedipus*. Trans. Robert Hurley, Mark Seem, and Helen R. Lane. London and New York: Continuum, 1983. p. 11.
77 Deleuze and Guattari, *Anti-Oedipus*. p. 9.

78 Gilles Deleuze, *Cinema 1: The Movement Image*. Trans. Hugh Tomlinson and Barbara Habberjam. London and New York: Continuum, 1986. p. 87.

79 Deleuze, *Cinema 1*. p. 89.

80 Francis Fukuyama, *End of History and the Last Man*. New York: Free Press, 1992. p. 46.

81 Luc Boltanski and Ève Chiapello. *The New Spirit of Capitalism*. Trans. Gregory Elliott. London and New York: Verso, 2005.

82 Clover, "Value | Crisis | Theory." p. 112.

83 Boltanski and Chiapello, *The New Spirit of Capitalism*. p. 379.

84 Stuart Gordon, *The Mammoth Book of Body Horror*. London: Robinson, 2012. Ebook

85 Matthew Pridham, "Underneath the Skin: John Carpenter's 'The Thing' and You." *Weird Fiction Review*. 25 March 2012. Web. 1 April 2016.

86 Adriana Cavarero, *Shocking Representation: Historical Trauma, National Cinema, and the Modern Film*. New York: Columbia UP, 2005. p. 146.

87 Jameson, *The Geopolitical Aesthetic: Cinema and Space in the World System*. Bloomington and Indianapolis: Indiana UP, 1992. p. 26.

88 Jameson, *The Geopolitical Aesthetic*. p. 26.

89 David Harvey, *A Brief History of Neoliberalism*. Oxford: Oxford UP, 2005. Ebook.

90 Patricia Allmer, "'Breaking in the Surface of the Real': The Discourses of Commodity Capitalism in Clive Barker's Hellraiser Narratives." *Space, Haunting, Discourse*. Eds. Maria Holmgren Troy and Elisabeth Wennö. Newcastle: Cambrdige Scholars Press, 2008. p. 20.

91 Zygmunt Bauman and Stanislaw Obirek. *On the World and Ourselves*. Trans. Lydia Bauman. Cambridge: Polity, 2015. p. 78. That combinatorial slash, which amalgamates Reagan and Thatcher into a single double-sexed entity, a beast with two backs, finds its appropriate realization in the mocked up cover image for the NOFX record "Ronnie and Mags." Go on, look it up.

92 Jean Baudrillard, *Cool Memories*. Trans. Chris Turner. London and New York: Verso, 1990. p. 5

93 Mark Kermode, *The Good, the Bad and the Multiplex: What's Wrong with Modern Movies?* London: Arrow Books, 2011. p. 92.

94 Jean-François Lyotard, *Libidinal Economy*. Trans. Iain Hamilton Grant. London and New York: Continuum, 1993. p. 1

95 Marx, *Capital*. pp. 416-7.

96 Philip Brophy, "Horrality – The Textuality of Contemporary Horror Films." *Screen* 27.1 (1986). p. 5.

97 Annie McClanahan, "Dead Pledges: Debt, Horror, and the Credit Crisis." *Post-45*. 5 July 2012. Web. 1 April 2016.

98 Alain Badiou, *Ethics: An Essay on the Understanding of Evil*. London: Verso, 2002. p. 122.

99 Luigi Zingales, Luigi Guiso, and Paola Sapienza. "Time Varying Risk Aversion." National Bureau of Economic Research. NBER Working Paper No. 19284. August 2013. Web. 1 April 2016.

100 Zingales, Guiso, and Sapienza. "Time Varying Risk Aversion."

101 Arrighi, *Adam Smith in Beijing: Lineages of the Twenty-first Century*. London and New York: Verso, 2007. p. 161.

102 Clover, "Value | Crisis | Theory." p. 113.

103 Guy Debord, *The Society of the Spectacle*. Trans. Donald Nicholson-Smith. New York: Zone Books, 1994. p. 12.

104 Robin Blackburn, "The Subprime Crisis." *New Left Review* 50 (March-April, 2008). p. 91.

105 David Edelstein, "Now Playing at Your Local Multiplex: Torture Porn." *New York Magazine*. 39.4. (6 February 2006). Web. 1 April 2016. For a cool essay on how Eli Roth updates the alignment of horror and porn in the era of multinational capitalism, see Maisha Wester, "Torture Porn and Uneasy Feminism: Re-thinking (Wo)men in Eli Roth's Hostel Films." *Quarterly Review of Film and Video* 29 (2012). pp. 387-400.

106 Edelstein, "Torture Porn."

107 Angela Ndalianis, *The Horror Sensorium: Media and the Senses*. Jefferson: McFarland and Company, 2012. p. 34.
108 Grant, *The Dread of Difference*. p. 307.
109 Aaron Michael Kerner, *Torture Porn in the Wake of 9/11: Horror, Exploitation, and the Cinema of Sensation*. New Brunswick: Rutgers UP, 2015. p. 131.
110 Slavoj Žižek, *The Parallax View*. Cambridge, MA: The MIT Press. p. 159.
111 Marx, *Capital*. p. 195.
112 Harvey, *The Enigma of Capital: and the Crises of Capitalism*. Oxford: Oxford, 2010. p. 1.
113 Franco "Bifo" Berardi, "Semio-capital and the problem of solidarity." *Through Europe*. 12 December 2012. Web. 1 April 2016.
114 Berardi, "Semio-capital and the problem of solidarity."
115 Costas Lapavitsas, *Profiting Without Producing: How Finance Exploits Us All*. London and New York: Verso, 2013. p. 326.
116 Simon Abrams, "The Human Centipede 3: Final Sequence." RogerEbert.com. 22 May 2015. Web. 1 April 2016.
117 Tom Six. "Tom Six sews up *The Human Centipede* | Interview (English version)." *Screen / Read*. 1 October 2010. Web. 1 April 2016.
118 Six, "Tom Six sews up *The Human Centipede*."
119 Reza Negarestani, "Will you be a part of it?" *Urbanomic*. 7 November 2013. Web. 1 April 2016.
120 BBFC. "Rejection Explanation: The Human Centipede 2 (Full Sequence)." n. d. Web. 1 April 2016.
121 Marx, *Capital*. p. 434.
122 Negarestani, "Will you be a part of it?" Ralph Jones, "'The Human Centipede 2' Is the Film That Made Me Love Life." *Vice*. 13 November 2013. Web. 1 April 2016.
123 André Bazin, *What is Cinema?* Trans. H. Gray. Berkeley: University of California Press, 1967. p. 15.

Repeater Books

is dedicated to the creation of a new reality. The landscape of twenty-first-century arts and letters is faded and inert, riven by fashionable cynicism, egotistical self-reference and a nostalgia for the recent past. Repeater intends to add its voice to those movements that wish to enter history and assert control over its currents, gathering together scattered and isolated voices with those who have already called for an escape from Capitalist Realism. Our desire is to publish in every sphere and genre, combining vigorous dissent and a pragmatic willingness to succeed where messianic abstraction and quiescent co-option have stalled: abstention is not an option: we are alive and we don't agree.